Prophecy Proof Insights on the Last Generation

Prophecy Proof Insights on the Last Generation

A Study on the Timing of Christ's Return

Wayne Croley

Prophecy Proof Insights Publications

Antelope

Prophecy Proof Insights on the Last Generation

© 2020 by Wayne Croley

All rights reserved. No part of this book may be reproduced or transmitted in any form or by any means, electronic or mechanical, including photocopying, recording, or by any information storage and retrieval system without the written permission of the publisher, except where permitted by law. For permission contact: permissions@prophecyproof.org

This book was written to educate people about Bible prophecy and end time events described in the Bible. However, it is not the ultimate authority on end time events and Bible prophecy. The Bible is the ultimate authority on end time events and Bible prophecy. This book's author *is not a prophet nor claims to be one*. The views expressed by the author in this book are based on his studies of the Bible.

The author and publisher will not be held liable or responsible for any choices or actions you make based on the information provided in this book. They will also not be held liable or responsible for any damages caused or alleged to be caused directly or indirectly by this book. You are responsible for your own choices, actions, and results.

Scripture taken from the King James Version.

eBook ISBN 13: 978-1-7322111-3-1

Print ISBN 13: 978-1-7322111-4-8

LCCN: 2020944795

Prophecy Proof Insights Publications

Antelope, CA

Dedication

I dedicate this book to my dad, Wayne M. Croley Sr., the man who introduced the subject of Bible prophecy to me.

My dad was a wonderful man and a great parent. I could fill a book praising how good of a man and parent he was.

I told my dad on his deathbed that I would write this book and dedicate it to him. I fulfill my promise to him with the publishing of this book.

Contents

Introduction — 1

Main Body

The Last Generation — 3
The Heavenly Signs — 10
Deceiving the Last Generation — 16
The 70 Weeks of Daniel — 22
The End Time Calendars — 36
Daniel's 2,300-Day Prophecy — 49
End Time Reckoning — 54

A Final Word — 70
Insights on the End Times — 71
Year By Year Timelines — 72
About the Author — 97

Introduction

We live in uncertain times. Many live in fear about what's coming next. We often hear about political strife, geopolitical tension, the spread of disease, and other unsettling news.

Many turn to Bible prophecy in search of answers to help us understand our chaotic world. Inevitably, some wonder whether we are the generation that will see the coming of Christ. Are we the last generation before the coming of Christ? Will we see all things that Christ told His disciples will come to pass?

People often ask me when I think the tribulation, the 7-year end time period, will begin. Many who ask me this question feel we are living in the last days.

I authored a book called *Prophecy Proof Insights of the End Times*. The purpose of that book was to provide readers with the startling truth about many end time events, including the Rapture, the great tribulation, and the rise of the Antichrist.

I did not give dates for end time events in *Prophecy Proof Insights of the End Times*. The reason I did not give dates is that I did not want to risk undermining the book in the years to come. I believe giving dates in *Prophecy Proof Insights of the End Times* could undermine how seriously people take that book if those dates pass and nothing happens.

Prophecy Proof Insights on the Last Generation is a much different book. In this book, I will give you plausible start dates and end dates for the tribulation and the Second Coming of Christ. I do not base my answers on pure speculation. Instead, I base my answers on research I have kept mostly quiet until now.

My dad, the man who introduced Bible prophecy to me, went to be with the Lord on June 16, 2020, after several months of dealing with several health issues. Until that point, my dad was the only man aware of the research I had done.

I told my dad about my research while on walks with him in 2019. My dad was struggling with the effects of a giant brain tumor that deprived him of much of his cognitive abilities. However, my dad had enough brain power left to grasp what I told him, and my findings impressed him.

I spent a lot of time with my dad at a skilled nursing facility after his brain surgery in January 2020. I told my dad I begun work on *Prophecy Proof Insights on the Last Generation* and I showed him a prototype for the book cover. My dad was so thrilled by this news that it may have been one of his proudest moments as a parent (possibly rivaling the time he held a copy of *Prophecy Proof Insights of the End Times* for the first time).

I knew at that point that I had to make my research findings public, but I did not know when I could make them public since I had to be with my dad as he tried to regain his health. However, my dad never fully recovered despite everyone's best efforts, including mine.

I visited my dad in ICU on June 15 and June 16, the day of his passing. I shared my heart with him and told him everything I wanted him to know before he left us. I promised my dad on his deathbed that I would publish *Prophecy Proof Insights on the Last Generation* and I would dedicate the book to him.

Therefore, I wrote this book with the goal of answering the question: "*Are we the last generation before the coming of Christ?*". Also, I wrote this book to fulfill a promise I gave my dad, a man who meant so much to me.

With that said, I hope that you will glean much from the research I have to share with you in this book.

The Last Generation

The term "last generation" stems from the Parable of the Fig Tree. This parable first appears in Matthew 24:32-25 (and also appears in Mark 13:28-31 and Luke 21:29-33). Here is the parable described in the Book of Matthew:

> Matthew 24:32-35
>
> (32) Now learn a parable of the fig tree; When his branch is yet tender, and putteth forth leaves, ye know that summer is nigh:
> (33) So likewise ye, when ye shall see all these things, know that it is near, even at the doors.
> (34) Verily I say unto you, This generation shall not pass, till all these things be fulfilled.
> (35) Heaven and earth shall pass away, but my words shall not pass away.

The Parable of the Fig Tree describes signs that people will see when Christ's coming nears. People who see the signs referred to in the parable are the last generation before the coming of Christ.

Some believe the Parable of the Fig Tree relates to Israel. Proponents argue that Israel represents the fig tree based on how some prophecies depict it as a fig tree and the creation of the state of Israel in 1948 ushered in the last generation.[1] This view has led to speculation over the past few decades about when Christ will return:

- One popular theory was that Christ would return in 1988. Proponents of this view believed a generation is 40 years.
- Some believed Christ would return in 2007. Proponents of this theory believed that 1967 marked the start of the last generation and a generation is 40 years.
- A recent theory posits that Christ will return between 2018 and 2028. Proponents argue that a generation is 70 to 80 years (based on Psalm 90:10) and the last generation started in 1948.

The Fig Tree & All the Trees

However, the Parable of the Fig Tree does not specifically relate to Israel because the parable is not solely about the fig tree. Luke 21:29 states the parable relates to the fig tree and *all the trees*:

> Luke 21:29-33
>
> (29) And he spake to them a parable; Behold the fig tree, and all the trees;
> (30) When they now shoot forth, ye see and know of your own selves that summer is now nigh at hand.
> (31) So likewise ye, when ye see these things come to pass, know ye that the kingdom of God is nigh at hand.
> (32) Verily I say unto you, This generation shall not pass away, till all be fulfilled.
> (33) Heaven and earth shall pass away: but my words shall not pass away.

The focus on the fig tree and *all the trees* suggests the parable is not solely about a development that relates to the fig tree. Israel may represent a fig tree, but the parable is not only about the fig tree sprouting leaves. The sprouting of *every tree*'s leaves, including the fig tree, is the focus of the parable as "they" are the subject of Luke 21:30.

Luke 21:29-33's account of the parable does not conflict with Matthew 24:32-35 and Mark 13:28-31. Matthew and Mark just emphasized the fig tree aspect of the parable (after all, the fig tree was distinguished from "all the trees" even in Luke 21:29-33).

The Parable's Purpose

Christ tried to convey the message that people can tell that His coming is near when they see the events He described taking place like people can tell that summer is near when they see trees sprout leaves.

In other words, Christ sought to alert people that the events He described are indicators that they can look at to gauge how near is His coming as they can look at the sprouting of leaves to tell what time of year it is.

Which events did Christ refer to in the Parable of the Fig Tree? Let's take a look.

The Olivet Discourse

The Parable of the Fig Tree is just one part of the Olivet Discourse, which Matthew 24, Mark 13, and Luke 21 cover. The Olivet Discourse records many key details about the coming end of the world that Christ gave.

Let's look at Matthew 24:3. Christ's disciples asked Him to tell them about the sign of His coming and the end of the world:

> Matthew 24:3
>
> And as he sat upon the mount of Olives, the disciples came unto him privately, saying, Tell us, when shall these things be? and what shall be the sign of thy coming, and of the end of the world?

Christ said the world would see:

- False Christs
- Wars
- Rumors of Wars
- Ethnic conflict
- Earthquakes
- Pestilence
- Famine
- Commotions (Luke 21:9)

Christ characterized these events as "the beginning of sorrows" or what many people call "birth pangs":

> Matthew 24:5-8
>
> (5) For many shall come in my name, saying, I am Christ; and shall deceive many.
> (6) And ye shall hear of wars and rumours of wars: see that ye be not troubled: for all these things must come to pass, but the end is not yet.
> (7) For nation shall rise against nation, and kingdom against kingdom: and there shall be famines, and pestilences, and earthquakes, in divers places.
> (8) All these are the beginning of sorrows.

Furthermore, Christ stressed that people should not be startled when these events transpire since they are preordained to occur before the end of the world. In fact, Christ qualified His statement by stating, "the end is not yet" when these events (false Christs, wars, rumors of war, etc.) occur.

The message to remain calm when birth pangs occur suggests that birth pangs will not occur only during the end times. As a result, the manifestation of birth pangs should not be a reason to reach drastic conclusions about the proximity of the end of the world. Therefore, it is fair to say that we are seeing birth pangs now.

The birth pangs analogy is important to understand as it may reveal how bad conditions may become in the future. Birth pangs begin with initial pain and followed by a period of relative calm. However, the frequency that pain is felt rises as time goes on.

Therefore, the frequency of the events that Christ described may rise as we near the tribulation. The frequency of war may rise, the frequency of revolutions may rise, etc.

The Great Tribulation

Christ later described the onset of a period known as the "great tribulation", which will begin when the Antichrist sets up an abomination of desolation, an object affront to God, in the Holy of Holies of the future Third Temple:[2]

> Matthew 24:15-16, 21-22
>
> (15) When ye therefore shall see the abomination of desolation, spoken of by Daniel the prophet, stand in the holy place, (whoso readeth, let him understand:)
> (16) Then let them which be in Judaea flee into the mountains:
>
> (21) For then shall be great tribulation, such as was not since the beginning of the world to this time, no, nor ever shall be.
> (22) And except those days should be shortened, there should no flesh be saved: but for the elect's sake those days shall be shortened.

The great tribulation will be the most trying time in history. The opponents of Antichrist will struggle to survive the persecution they will face, but not everyone will die.

The End of the Tribulation

Christ described several heavenly signs that will appear after the end of the great tribulation. He revealed that He will come after these signs appear:

> Matthew 24:29-31
>
> (29) Immediately after the tribulation of those days shall the sun be darkened, and the moon shall not give her light, and the stars shall fall from heaven, and the powers of the heavens shall be shaken:
> (30) And then shall appear the sign of the Son of man in heaven: and then shall all the tribes of the earth mourn, and they shall see the Son of man coming in the clouds of heaven with power and great glory.
> (31) And he shall send his angels with a great sound of a trumpet, and they shall gather together his elect from the four winds, from one end of heaven to the other.

Christ shared the Parable of the Fig Tree after He described the heavenly signs heralding His coming.

I believe these heavenly signs are what Christ alluded to in the Parable of the Fig Tree. People who follow Christ's teachings will know that His coming is near when the heavenly signs preceding His arrival appear. This is like how people know that summer is near when the fig tree and all trees sprout their leaves.

Therefore, the last generation will see the heavenly signs that Christ told His disciples about and many of the events He spoke of in the Olivet Discourse.

Even with the Parable of the Fig Tree not referring to the creation of the state of Israel in 1948, is it still possible for the generation that saw its creation to be the last generation? We will find out in coming chapters.

Notes

1. Proponents of the idea that the Parable of the Fig Tree is about Israel cite several passages to make their case, including Jeremiah 24:1-9, Hosea 9:10, and Mark 11:13-23.
2. I do not want to confuse you. The tribulation refers to a 7-year end time period. The "great tribulation" is a period of intense persecution within that 7-year period.

The Heavenly Signs

We saw in the last chapter how the last generation will see the heavenly signs that will herald Christ's coming. As a result, many people watch the heavens in search of the signs that Christ spoke of.

Over the years, I have noticed how expectations for Christ's return tend to rise near the time of a major lunar eclipse. The reason for this rise is that the Bible describes how the sun and the moon's appearance will change just before Christ comes:

- The sun will darken.
- The moon will resemble blood. Many call this a "blood moon".
- Both events often take place at the time of a lunar eclipse.

We know the dates of many future blood moon or lunar eclipse events. Some have used these dates to predict when Christ will come.

Should we use the dates of future lunar eclipses to forecast when Christ will come? We will answer this key question in this chapter.

After the Tribulation

Recall that Christ said that the heavenly signs will not appear until the great tribulation, the worst persecution in history, ends:

> Matthew 24:29-30
>
> (29) Immediately after the tribulation of those days shall the sun be darkened, and the moon shall not give her light, and the stars shall fall from heaven, and the powers of the heavens

shall be shaken:
(30) And then shall appear the sign of the Son of man in heaven: and then shall all the tribes of the earth mourn, and they shall see the Son of man coming in the clouds of heaven with power and great glory.

We will see later in this book that this persecution will not begin until 3.5 years through the tribulation. We are not in the tribulation yet, so any prediction about Christ's coming based on a lunar eclipse date in the next 3.5 years will fail.

What about predictions based on lunar eclipse dates more than 3.5 years from now? Let's look at what else is taking place in the world when the heavenly signs appear.

The Gathering of Armies

Joel 3 gives us a key detail about the time when the heavenly signs will appear. The chapter tells us that all nations will have already assembled near Jerusalem for battle when the signs appear:

> Joel 3:1-2, 12-16
>
> (1) For, behold, in those days, and in that time, when I shall bring again the captivity of Judah and Jerusalem,
> (2) **I will also gather all nations, and will bring them down into the valley of Jehoshaphat, and will plead with them there** for my people and for my heritage Israel, whom they have scattered among the nations, and parted my land.
> ...
> (12) **Let the heathen be wakened, and come up to the valley of Jehoshaphat: for there will I sit to judge all the heathen round about.**
> (13) Put ye in the sickle, for the harvest is ripe: come, get you down; for the press is full, the fats overflow; for their wickedness is great.
> (14) **Multitudes, multitudes in the valley of decision**: for the

day of the Lord is near in the valley of decision.
(15) **The sun and the moon shall be darkened, and the stars shall withdraw their shining.**
(16) The Lord also shall roar out of Zion, and utter his voice from Jerusalem; and the heavens and the earth shall shake: but the Lord will be the hope of his people, and the strength of the children of Israel.

This detail tells us we must see all the nations of the earth gather near Jerusalem for battle before the heavenly signs will appear. Many miss this key point when they consider predictions based on lunar eclipse dates.

The 6th Seal

The Book of Revelation describes 7 seals on the outside of a scroll that only Christ is worthy to open. Revelation 6 describes events that will take place during the end times as Christ opens the seals. A new series of events will take place each time He opens a seal.

The opening of the 6th seal introduces a series of events that will include the appearance of the heavenly signs that Christ spoke of:

Revelation 6:12-17

(12) And I beheld when he had opened the sixth seal, and, lo, there was a great earthquake; and the **sun became black as sackcloth of hair, and the moon became as blood;**
(13) **And the stars of heaven fell unto the earth, even as a fig tree casteth her untimely figs, when she is shaken of a mighty wind.**
(14) **And the heaven departed as a scroll when it is rolled together**; and every mountain and island were moved out of their places.
(15) And the kings of the earth, and the great men, and the rich men, and the chief captains, and the mighty men, and every bondman, and every free man, hid themselves in the dens and

in the rocks of the mountains;
(16) And said to the mountains and rocks, Fall on us, and hide us from the face of him that sitteth on the throne, and from the wrath of the Lamb:
(17) For the great day of his wrath is come; and who shall be able to stand?

Isaiah 2 and Luke 21 also describe these events:

Isaiah 2:10, 19

(10) Enter into the rock, and hide thee in the dust, **for fear of the Lord, and for the glory of his majesty.**
...
(19) And they shall go into the holes of the rocks, and into the caves of the earth, **for fear of the Lord, and for the glory of his majesty, when he ariseth to shake terribly the earth.**

Luke 21:25-27

(25) And there shall be signs in the sun, and in the moon, and in the stars; and upon the earth distress of nations, with perplexity; the sea and the waves roaring;
(26) **Men's hearts failing them for fear, and for looking after those things which are coming on the earth: for the powers of heaven shall be shaken.**
(27) And then shall **they see the Son of man coming in a cloud with power and great glory.**

These passages describe people seeking refuge because they are terrified by what they see. They will see much more than the sun and the moon darken when they look to the heavens:

- The signs will also appear in the stars. The stars will look like they are falling from the sky.
- People may see a heavenly dimension that we now cannot see as the sky recedes like a scroll.
- People may even see a manifestation of God and His Son when that dimension opens.

The signs in the heavens will come at a time when the Lord will unveil His majesty for the world to see. The signs in the heavens will go far beyond what any lunar eclipse can bring. These facts suggest that the appearance of the heavenly signs is unrelated to a lunar eclipse.

Pillars of Smoke

Joel 2 gives us a good clue about how a blood moon can appear without a lunar eclipse. The chapter tells us that a lot of smoke will be present in the skies at that time:

> Joel 2:30-31
>
> (30) And I will shew wonders in the heavens and in the earth, **blood, and fire, and pillars of smoke.**
> (31) The sun shall be turned into darkness, and the moon into blood, before the great and terrible day of the Lord come.

Smoke can alter the appearance of the moon in the sky. In fact, blood moons often appear after a volcanic eruption or the outbreak of a major wildfire. I have witnessed blood moons in the sky when large fires burn near where I live.

The great earthquake (Revelation 6:12), fire, and the pillars of smoke (Joel 2:30) indicate that there will be huge geological instability around the world just before Christ comes. We can deduce from this that it is likely that:

- Many volcanoes will erupt and send lots of smoke and other particles into the atmosphere.
- Smoke and particles from these eruptions could cover the world.
- The blood moon caused by these eruptions will appear across the world.

Therefore, a blood moon can easily appear at that time with no lunar eclipse.

Can We Rely on Lunar Eclipse Dates?

Given all that we've seen in this chapter, I would not rely on the dates of future lunar eclipses to forecast when Christ will return. The heavenly signs will appear as part of the Lord unveiling His full majesty to the people of the earth. The grandeur of these signs will go far beyond what any lunar eclipse can show. Therefore, the change in the sun and the moon's appearance is unlikely to come from a lunar eclipse.

We will next look at another event that will have a big impact on those living in the last generation.

Deceiving the Last Generation

The Antichrist will play a key role during the time of the last generation. He will oversee a kingdom that will dominate the world (Daniel 7:23-25 and Revelation 13:7).

The Antichrist will work at a time when Satan shall unleash all his lying signs and wonders (2 Thessalonians 2:9). I believe Satan's biggest end time deception will be to make the people of Earth believe that the Antichrist will be resurrected from the dead.

I will explain why the Antichrist will appear as someone resurrected from the dead and why many will fall for this deception in this chapter.

The Beast of Revelation 17

John, the author of the Book of Revelation, described three creatures with seven heads and ten horns:

- The dragon of Revelation 12 represents Satan.
- The beast of Revelation 13 represents the empire of the Antichrist.
- The beast of Revelation 17 represents the Antichrist.

The ten horns of the beast of Revelation 17 represent ten kings that will surrender their power to the Antichrist during his reign (Revelation 17:12-13).

The seven heads of the beast of Revelation 17 equate to seven mountains, and these relate to seven kings. Five kings came before John's time, one king was in power during John's time, and the other had not yet appear on Earth:

Revelation 17:9-10

> (9) And here is the mind which hath wisdom. The seven heads are seven mountains, on which the woman sitteth.
> (10) And there are seven kings: five are fallen, and one is, and the other is not yet come; and when he cometh, he must continue a short space.

Verse 11 tells us that the beast of Revelation 17 represents an eighth king. The verse also reveals the importance of the seven kings, which is that one of the kings will serve *again* as the eighth king:

> And the beast that was, and is not, even he is the eighth, and is of the seven, and goeth into perdition.

Therefore, the Antichrist will be a leader who returns to power. We will see that he will return to power after being brought back to life.

The False Resurrection

Revelation 17:8 describes the beast as the one who "was, and is not, and yet is" when viewed by the inhabitants of the earth:

> The beast that thou sawest was, and is not; and shall ascend out of the bottomless pit, and go into perdition: and they that dwell on the earth shall wonder, whose names were not written in the book of life from the foundation of the world, when they behold the beast that was, and is not, and yet is.

In the vision (which is being viewed from the perspective of those living in the future), the beast once lived (was). However, there is a paradox in phrasing because:

- The beast also "is not", which indicates that the beast is not alive.
- And the beast "yet is", which indicates that the beast is alive.

This description differs from how Revelation 4:8 describes God who lives forever: ("which was, and is, and is to come"):

> And the four beasts had each of them six wings about him; and they were full of eyes within: and they rest not day and night, saying, Holy, holy, holy, Lord God Almighty, which was, and is, and is to come.

The beast ascends from the bottomless pit, a place described by the Bible where wicked souls go; his soul leaves the bottomless pit. At first glance, we could compare this event to the resurrection of Jesus Christ:

> Acts 2:31
>
> He seeing this before spake of the resurrection of Christ, that his soul was not left in hell, neither his flesh did see corruption.

Christ vs. Antichrist

To compare the resurrection of Christ to the accession of the beast, we need to look at Revelation 1:18 where Christ said:

> I am he that liveth, and was dead; and, behold, I am alive for evermore, Amen; and have the keys of hell and of death.

The beast and Christ will have both faced temporary death as one already rose from it and another is foretold to rise from it. However, the beast's condition when he returns to Earth will differ greatly from when Jesus returned.

- Jesus is alive and will live forever.
- The beast "is not" and "yet is".

The paradox of living for the beast suggests he will not perform a real resurrection. Though the beast appears on the earth after rising from the bottomless pit, he cannot do what Jesus did.

A consequence of this false rise is that the beast can only be on Earth for a short time after his return.

- The beast "is", but not always will be; the beast will head to his destruction.
- In contrast, Christ taught that those who are truly resurrected will not die again:

    Luke 20:35-36

    (35) But they which shall be accounted worthy to obtain that world, and the resurrection from the dead, neither marry, nor are given in marriage:
    (36) Neither can they die any more: for they are equal unto the angels; and are the children of God, being the children of the resurrection.

Therefore, we can glean from Revelation 17 that Antichrist will appear as if he's been resurrected from the dead. He will not truly be resurrected, but it will look like he is.

Other Factors to Consider

Beyond the beast of Revelation 17's description, how else can we tell that the Antichrist will appear like he's been resurrected from the dead? Let's consider two other details.

The Fatal Wound

The beast of Revelation 13 represents the empire of the Antichrist, but its actions mirror the actions of the Antichrist as he oversees his empire. Revelation 13 twice states that one of the beast's heads will recover after being slain:

Revelation 13:3

And I saw **one of his heads as it were wounded to death; and his deadly wound was healed:** and all the world wondered after the beast.

Revelation 13:14

And deceiveth them that dwell on the earth by the means of those miracles which he had power to do in the sight of the beast; saying to them that dwell on the earth, that they should make an image to **the beast, which had the wound by a sword, and did live.**

These verses refer to the restoration of the Antichrist since people will make and worship images of him after his recovery (Revelation 13:14-15).

People Will Marvel at Antichrist

Christians must put their faith in the resurrection of Christ and ask skeptics to have faith in it as well since we do not have physical proof (like a photo or video) showing that Christ rose from the dead.

The Antichrist will not have the same challenge that Christians face to gain followers. He will deceive many people into thinking he's been resurrected from the dead through his physical return. He may get even the most skeptical people to believe in him and view him as an object of worship.

The beast will amaze many people according to Revelation 17:8. The beast will be visible to everyone on the earth because he will ascend from the bottomless pit and live. Those whose names are not in the Book of Life shall marvel at the beast.

From these people's perspective, the beast is what Christians believe Jesus to be: someone who died and rose from the dead. To capture this perspective, many people will ask: "Who is like unto the beast? who is able to make war with him?" (Revelation 13:4)

Let's Pause for a Moment

I argued that the false resurrection of the Antichrist will be Satan's biggest end time deception. Many people will fall prey to this deception and will worship the Antichrist like he is a god during the time of the last generation.

I am not 100% sure how Satan will stage this end time deception as this is his biggest one. Satan would likely want to keep details regarding this deception a secret because so much is at stake.

The reason I devoted a chapter to the false resurrection of the Antichrist will become clear later in this book. I will refer to this chapter again, so make sure you have a firm grasp of it before continuing.

The 70 Weeks of Daniel

The 70 weeks of Daniel is an important timeline to learn about. Learning this timeline will help you a lot. You will gain critical knowledge about the end times. You will also gain an appreciation of how powerful and precise Bible prophecy is.

In this chapter, I show how Daniel's first 69 weeks have already transpired and I outline the upcoming 70th week of Daniel.

The Vision

The Angel Gabriel appeared to the Prophet Daniel as he prayed to God. Gabriel told Daniel that 70 weeks were given to the people of Israel and the city of Jerusalem to bring about several developments:

> Daniel 9:24
>
> Seventy weeks are determined upon thy people and upon thy holy city, to finish the transgression, and to make an end of sins, and to make reconciliation for iniquity, and to bring in everlasting righteousness, and to seal up the vision and prophecy, and to anoint the most Holy.

Here is an overview of the developments that will begin to be brought about at the completion of the 70th week of Daniel:

- **Finish the Transgression:** The Hebrew word for "transgression" (*pesha`*) implies "revolt" or "rebellion" at a national level.[1] The idea is that Israel's national rebellion against the Lord will come to an end.
- **Make an End of Sins:** The Hebrew word for "end" (*chatham*) implies "to close up" or "to seal".[2] The idea is not that all sin will be put to an end so that no one will ever sin again after the 70th week of Daniel. The idea is that Israel's sins will be removed from sight or concealed.
- **Make Reconciliation for Iniquity:** The Hebrew word for "reconciliation" (*kaphar*) implies atonement.[3] The idea is Israel's iniquity will be atone for.
- **Bring in Everlasting Righteousness:** Everlasting righteousness will begin with the establishment of God and Christ's eternal reign (Daniel 7:27 and Revelation 11:15-18).
- **Seal Up Vision and Prophecy:** The Hebrew word *chatham* appears again here, which suggests that something will be closed up or sealed. In this context, the vision and prophecy will be preserved through time.[4]
- **Anoint the Most Holy:** This likely refers to the crowning of Christ as the King of the earth (Revelation 11:15-18) or the consecration of a temple, the Millennium temple, which Christ will set up (Zechariah 6:13).

The First 69 Weeks of Daniel

Gabriel gave Daniel details about the first 69 weeks:

- The first week would begin with a call to restore and build Jerusalem.
- The restoration and building process would last for 7 weeks, and after that, there would be an additional 62 weeks ending when the Messiah (Christ) is "cut off".

This 69 week time frame saw its fulfillment nearly 2,000 years ago with Christ's crucifixion and ascension to Heaven:

Daniel 9:25-26

(25) Know therefore and understand, that from the going forth of the commandment to restore and to build Jerusalem unto the Messiah the Prince shall be seven weeks, and threescore and two weeks: the street shall be built again, and the wall, even in troublous times.
(26) And after threescore and two weeks shall Messiah be cut off, but not for himself: and the people of the prince that shall come shall destroy the city and the sanctuary; and the end thereof shall be with a flood, and unto the end of the war desolations are determined.

Jerusalem was in ruins long before the time Daniel received the vision in the 6th century B.C. The call to restore Jerusalem that Gabriel spoke of came in the Hebrew month of Nisan during Artaxerxes's 20th year of the reign:

Nehemiah 2:1, 5

(1) And it came to pass in the month Nisan, in the twentieth year of Artaxerxes the king, that wine was before him: and I took up the wine, and gave it unto the king. Now I had not been beforetime sad in his presence.

(5) And I said unto the king, If it please the king, and if thy servant have found favour in thy sight, that thou wouldest send me unto Judah, unto the city of my fathers' sepulchres, that I may build it.

Most scholars agree that the 20th year of Artaxerxes was in 445 or 444 B.C. while Christ's crucifixion occurred between 26 and 36 A.D.-corresponding to the rule of Pontius Pilate.

The Prophetic Week

Gabriel did not speak of 70 weeks where each week is 7 days long. The Hebrew rendering of the word "week" in Daniel is *shabuwa`*, which means "seven".[5] Therefore we can also refer to Daniel's prophecy as "the 70 sevens".

We can derive the length of a prophetic week by analyzing the structure of the 70th week of Daniel. Daniel's 70th week has two distinct halves.

The Antichrist will confirm a covenant with many at the start of the week, but will halt the daily sacrifice midway through the week:

> Daniel 9:27
>
> And he shall confirm the covenant with many for one week: and in the midst of the week he shall cause the sacrifice and the oblation to cease, and for the overspreading of abominations he shall make it desolate, even until the consummation, and that determined shall be poured upon the desolate.

The second half of the week will be a period of severe persecution. This period will last for "time, times, and an half" according to Daniel 12:7: "it shall be for a time, times, and an half; and when he shall have accomplished to scatter the power of the holy people, all these things shall be finished."

The word "time" is translated from the Hebrew word *mow`ed*, which can mean "a year".[6] Most commentators that analyze Daniel's 70 weeks prophecy correctly agree that "time, times, and an half" represents 3.5 years. Therefore, a prophetic week is a 7-year period with dual 3.5-year halves.

We learn that 3.5 prophetic years (or half of a prophetic week) is equivalent to 1,260 days by comparing Revelation 12:14 and 12:6, and if we divide 1,260 days by 3.5 years we find that a prophetic year is 360 days long:

> Revelation 12:14
>
> And to the woman were given two wings of a great eagle, that she might fly into the wilderness, into her place, where she is nourished for **a time, and times, and half a time**, from the face of the serpent.
>
> Revelation 12:6
>
> And the woman fled into the wilderness, where she hath a place prepared of God, that they should feed her there **a thousand two hundred and threescore days.**

Given that one-half of a prophetic week is 1,260 days, we can conclude that a whole prophetic week is 2,520 days.

Attempts to Verify the Prophecy

Many have tried to show the precision of the first 69 weeks of the prophecy. Sir Robert Anderson and Harold Hoehner wrote two of the most famous efforts to verify the prophecy.

Sir Robert Anderson

Sir Robert Anderson wrote about the coming of Christ in his book *The Coming Prince*. Anderson gave great insight about the 70 weeks prophecy and showed us how to calculate a prophetic year.

He set March 14, 445 B.C. on the Julian calendar (March 9, 445 B.C. on our calendar) as the start date of the first week of Daniel and April 6, 32 A.D. on the Julian calendar (April 4, 32 A.D. on our calendar and Palm Sunday) as the end date of the 69th week of

Daniel. Anderson claimed that 32 A.D. was likely the termination year since Passover occurred on a Thursday.

Anderson's timeline was flawed since Passover fell on a Monday in 32 A.D., a day of the week that would not work as the crucifixion date. Despite this issue, Anderson's work paved the way for others.

Harold Hoehner

Harold Hoehner wrote the acclaimed book *Chronological Aspects of the Life of Christ*. Hoehner knew that Anderson's end date did not work, so he aimed for 33 A.D.

Hoehner's proposed 69 week time frame has March 5, 444 B.C. on the Julian calendar (February 28, 444 B.C. on our calendar) as the start of the first week of Daniel and March 30, 33 A.D. on the Julian calendar (March 28, 33 A.D. on our calendar) as the end date of Daniel's 69th week.

Hoehner's study has two major flaws. First, his start date for Daniel's first week is impossible.

- The only source that Hoehner cited to support his start date was Herman H. Goldstine's *New and Full Moons, 1001 B.C. to A.D. 1651*, which listed the dates when a new moon was present. The issue with this source is that although a Hebrew month begins at the appearance of the new moon, Goldstine did not indicate which Hebrew month it was when each new moon appeared. March 5, 444 B.C. occurred in the early portion of the Hebrew month of Adar II since 444 B.C. had an additional month due to it being a leap year on the Hebrew calendar.

Second, the 69 week timeline Hoehner proposed does not span the total length of 69 prophetic weeks.

My Attempt to Verify the Prophecy

I used a calendar converter found at Abdicate.net to find the start date and end date of Daniel's first 69 weeks.[7] The calendar gives dates for:

- The Jewish (Hebrew) calendar
- The Gregorian calendar: The calendar system we use today.
- The Julian calendar: A calendar system used by astronomers to perform arithmetic with dates.

The calendar converter also accounts for the absence of a year 0 in history and can calculate the difference between dates.

Before I show the results, here are the conditions that the proposed 69 weeks of Daniel time frame must meet:

- The start of the first week must be in the month of Nisan in either 445 or 444 B.C.
- The year of Christ's crucifixion must occur between 26-36 A.D.
- Christ's crucifixion date must fall on the 14th of Nisan (eve of Passover) and fall on a Friday.[8]
- The end of the 69th week took place at the ascension of Christ rather than the crucifixion of Christ since His removal from the world occurred at His ascension.[9]
- Christ rose from the dead on Sunday and spent 40 days on Earth before He ascended to Heaven (Acts 1:1-3, 9-11).

33 A.D. is the only year among the three years from 26-36 A.D. that had Nisan 14 on a Friday (26, 33, and 36 A.D.) and could comply with the conditions set:

- Nisan 14, 33 A.D. occurred on April 1 of the Gregorian calendar.
- Sunday, April 3 or Nisan 16 was the date of Christ's resurrection.
- Christ's ascension date (the end of the 69th week) occurred 40 days later (counting the resurrection date as the first day) on May 12, 33 A.D.

I converted 69 prophetic weeks into days to begin the search for the start of the first week of Daniel. I did this by turning 69 prophetic weeks into prophetic years and then prophetic years into days:

- One Prophetic Week = 7 Prophetic Years
- 69 Weeks of 7 Prophetic Years = 483 Prophetic Years
- One Prophetic Year = 360 Days
- 483 Prophetic Years x 360 Days in a Prophetic Year = 173,880 Days

According to the calendar converter, 173,380 days from May 12, 33 A.D. was April 18, 444 B.C. The key dates of this proposed time frame are in Figure 1:

Figure 1: The 69 Weeks Time Frame

Crucifixion: April 1, 33 A.D. or

Nisan 14, 3793 (Hebrew) or April 3, 33 A.D. (Julian)

Resurrection: April 3, 33 A.D. or

Nisan 16, 3793 (Hebrew) or April 5, 33 A.D. (Julian)

Ascension: May 12, 33 A.D. or

Iyyar 25, 3793 (Hebrew) or May 14, 33 A.D. (Julian)

The Start of the 1st Week: April 18, 444 B.C.

Nisan 22, 3317 (Hebrew) or April 23, 444 B.C. (Julian)

Therefore, Christ was "cut off" on May 12, 33 A.D., which was 483 prophetic years or exactly 69 prophetic weeks after the decree came to restore Jerusalem on April 18, 444 B.C.

Thus, Daniel's 69 week time frame complies with Scripture when Christ's ascension marks the end of the 69th week instead of His crucifixion:

- This is a bittersweet trade-off because we cannot claim that Daniel 9 predicted that Christ, the Messiah, would be crucified at the end of Daniel's 69th week.
- However, we can still proclaim that Jesus Christ is the Messiah because the prophecy referred to Him as having that role.
- Also, we gain precision that reveals Christ's likely crucifixion date and precision that enables us to dispel critics about the prophecy's accuracy.

The Rest of the Prophecy

The prophecy next called for the destruction of Jerusalem and the Second Temple. Both events occurred in 70 A.D.:

> Daniel 9:26
>
> And after threescore and two weeks shall Messiah be cut off, but not for himself: and the people of the prince that shall come shall destroy the city and the sanctuary; and the end thereof shall be with a flood, and unto the end of the war desolations are determined.

The 70th Week of Daniel

The 70th week of Daniel will be a key time when many end time events will transpire. This final 7-year period (also known as "the tribulation") will start with the confirmation of a covenant with many. However, halfway through the week (3.5 years thru) the Antichrist will stop the daily sacrifice in the future Third Temple. He will also set up an abomination of desolation, an object affront to God, in the temple:

Daniel 9:27

And he shall confirm the covenant with many for one week: and in the midst of the week he shall cause the sacrifice and the oblation to cease, and for the overspreading of abominations he shall make it desolate, even until the consummation, and that determined shall be poured upon the desolate.

Recall that Christ warned that a time of great tribulation will begin after the abomination of desolation is set up (Matthew 24:15-21). Indeed, a man clothed in linen told Daniel that the people of Israel will face unprecedented trouble for 3.5 years, or a time (year), times (two years), and half a time (half a year):

Daniel 12:1, 6-7

(1) And at that time shall Michael stand up, the great prince which standeth for the children of thy people: and there shall be a time of trouble, such as never was since there was a nation even to that same time: and at that time thy people shall be delivered, every one that shall be found written in the book.

(6) And one said to the man clothed in linen, which was upon the waters of the river, How long shall it be to the end of these wonders?
(7) And I heard the man clothed in linen, which was upon the waters of the river, when he held up his right hand and his left hand unto heaven, and sware by him that liveth for ever that it shall be for a time, times, and an half; and when he shall have accomplished to scatter the power of the holy people, all these things shall be finished.

Therefore, the second half of the 70th week of Daniel will be a time of great persecution.

Let's Pause for a Moment

The Lord has an ongoing plan to redeem the people of Israel. We can see this plan in motion through the 70 weeks of Daniel prophecy. With 69 weeks completed, we await the start of the 70th week of Daniel.

I know this chapter contained a lot of information. I encourage you to reread any parts of this chapter that you may not fully understand. It's important that you understand this prophecy because I will refer to it a lot in the remaining chapters.

Notes

1. Strong, James. "pesha`". *Strong's Exhaustive Concordance of the Bible*. New York, Cincinnati, Eaton & Mains; Jennings & Graham, 1890. H6588.
2. Ibid. "chatham". H2856.
3. Ibid. "kaphar". H3722.
4. Some argue that sealing up vision and prophecy implies that all prophecy will be confirmed to be true or that vision and prophecy will no longer be needed. However, I am skeptical of this view. The reason is that the young men of Israel will have visions, and the sons and daughters of Israel will prophesy after the Lord pours out His Spirit on all flesh (Joel 2:26-28). This will take place after they gather in the land of Israel following the end of the war of Armageddon.
5. Strong, James. "shabuwa`". *Strong's Exhaustive Concordance of the Bible*. New York, Cincinnati, Eaton & Mains; Jennings & Graham, 1890. H7620.
6. Ibid. "mow`ed". H4150.
7. "Jewish Calendar, Gregorian Calendar, and Julian Calendar Converter." *The Shepherd's Page*. 2020. Web. 7 Aug. 2020. http://abdicate.net/cal.aspx.
8. Some believe the crucifixion of Christ took place on a Wednesday instead of a Friday. I have studied both dates, and after studying the issue, I believe the crucifixion most likely took place on a Friday.

The Bible states that the crucifixion of Christ took place on the day of preparation, a term directly connected to Friday-the day before the weekly Sabbath (Mark 15:42, Luke 23:54, John 19:31).

Nevertheless, Wednesday proponents will argue that Christ's crucifixion could not occur on a Friday because Christ said He would spend "three days and three nights in the heart of the earth":

> Matthew 12:40
> For as Jonas was three days and three nights in the whale's belly; so shall the Son of man be three days and three nights in the heart of the earth.

However, the term "three days and three nights" was not a phrase that signified 72 hours. The term was an idiom whose basic meaning in New Testament days was equivalent to the meaning of the term "day after tomorrow" nowadays.

We can see that "three days and three nights" does not equate to a literal 72-hour period by looking at a comparable term: "the third day". Christ told His followers that He would rise from the dead on "the third day":

> Mark 10:33-34
> (33) Saying, Behold, we go up to Jerusalem; and the Son of man shall be delivered unto the chief priests, and unto the scribes; and they shall condemn him to death, and shall deliver him to the Gentiles: (34) And they shall mock him, and shall scourge him, and shall spit upon him, and shall kill him: and the third day he shall rise again.

The "third day" is comparable to "three days and three nights" because they both represent the amount of time that Christ would be dead. "The third day" does not represent a literal 72-hour period. In fact, Luke 13:32 strongly suggests that "the third day" covers a span of time equivalent to the day after tomorrow:

> Luke 13:32
> And he said unto them, Go ye, and tell that fox, Behold, I cast out devils, and I do cures to day and to morrow, and the third day I shall be perfected.

Given all this, we can conclude that the term "three days and three nights" is equivalent to the day after tomorrow.

9. It would be great to prove that Daniel's 69th week finished on the exact date of Christ's crucifixion. However, this is problematic since subtract-

ing 173,880 days from the crucifixion of Christ will not place the start date of the first week of Daniel in the month of Nisan. Given this, we must look for another way to make the time frame fit between Nisan of Artaxerxes's 20th year and the date that the Messiah was "cut-off".

Many believe the term "cut-off" in Daniel 9:26 refers to Christ's crucifixion. This is why most attempts to show the precision of Daniel's 69 week timeline focus on Christ's crucifixion date. However, I believe the term "cut-off" refers to Christ temporarily being taken away without His kingdom when He ascended to Heaven.

According to Keil and Delitzsch, the term "cut-off" (Hebrew: יכרת) does not necessarily refer to the death of the Messiah:

> "... יכרת does not denote the putting to death, or cutting off of existence, but only the annihilation of His place as *Maschiach* among His people and in His kingdom. For if after His "cutting off" He has not what He should have, it is clear that annihilation does not apply to Him personally, but only that He has lost His place and function as the *Maschiach*." (Delitzsch, Franz, and Carl F. Keil. *Biblical Commentary on the Old Testament*. The Book of the Prophet Daniel. Translated by M.G. Easton. Edinburgh: T. & T. Clark, 1884. 361-362.)

Many Jews view the Messiah as a leader who will bring world peace, gather the people of Israel back to the land of Israel, and restore the Kingdom of Israel. Christ said just before His ascension that it was not yet time for Him to set up the Messianic Kingdom of Israel:

> Acts 1:6-7
> (6) When they therefore were come together, they asked of him, saying, Lord, wilt thou at this time restore again the kingdom to Israel?
> (7) And he said unto them, It is not for you to know the times or the seasons, which the Father hath put in his own power.

Therefore, Christ was not meant to serve as a messianic ruler in His first coming. He will have a messianic kingdom in the future since Gabriel called Him the Messiah.

The notion that the Messiah would temporarily go away without His kingdom is not blasphemy!!! In fact, Revelation 12:5 described Christ, the future ruler of all the nations, being taken up to Heaven:

> And she brought forth a man child, who was to rule all nations with a rod of iron: and her child was caught up unto God, and to his throne.

Finally, the interpretation of "cut off" that I present makes further sense when you consider the next phrase in Daniel 9:26. The next phrase reads "...but not for himself". This phrase relates to the fact that Christ left Earth without His messianic kingdom.

With "cut-off" not referring to Christ's crucifixion, we can reference His ascension date as the date when He was cut-off.

The End Time Calendars

The Book of Daniel introduces us to several timelines that encompass various end time events. For instance, we learned about the 70 weeks of Daniel prophecy and the 70th week of Daniel in Daniel 9.

In this chapter, we will look at the timing of several other key end time events alluded to in the Book of Daniel and elsewhere.

The Abomination of Desolation

Recall that the Antichrist will stop the daily sacrifice and set up the abomination of desolation, an object affront to God, at the midpoint of the 70th week (or 1,260 days since its start):

> Daniel 9:27
>
> And he shall confirm the covenant with many for one week: **and in the midst of the week he shall cause the sacrifice and the oblation to cease, and for the overspreading of abominations he shall make it desolate**, even until the consummation, and that determined shall be poured upon the desolate.

We can glean more insight about what will happen when the Antichrist sets up the abomination of desolation. The Apostle Paul wrote that the Antichrist would sit in the temple of God (in Jerusalem) and proclaim that he is God. The Antichrist's true identity as the "man of sin" shall be revealed at that moment:

> 2 Thessalonians 2:1-4
>
> (1) Now we beseech you, brethren, by the coming of our Lord Jesus Christ, and by our gathering together unto him,

(2) That ye be not soon shaken in mind, or be troubled, neither by spirit, nor by word, nor by letter as from us, as that the day of Christ is at hand.
(3) Let no man deceive you by any means: for that day shall not come, except there come a falling away first, and that man of sin be revealed, the son of perdition.
(4) Who opposeth and exalteth himself above all that is called God, or that is worshipped; so that he as God sitteth in the temple of God, shewing himself that he is God.

Daniel 11:36-39 most likely describes the Antichrist when he sets up the abomination of desolation. Like 2 Thessalonians 2:4, Daniel 11:36-37 describes the Antichrist as he exalts himself above all things:

Daniel 11:36-37

(36) **And the king shall do according to his will; and he shall exalt himself, and magnify himself above every god**, and shall speak marvellous things against the God of gods, and shall prosper till the indignation be accomplished: for that that is determined shall be done.
(37) **Neither shall he regard the God of his fathers, nor the desire of women, nor regard any god: for he shall magnify himself above all.**

2 Thessalonians 2:4

Who opposeth and **exalteth himself above all that is called God, or that is worshipped; so that he as God sitteth in the temple of God, shewing himself that he is God.**

The "God of Forces"

Although the Antichrist will magnify himself above God, Daniel 11:38 states that the Antichrist will honor an entity known as the "god of forces", a god whom his fathers did not know, with riches:

> But in his estate shall he honour the God of forces: and a god whom his fathers knew not shall he honour with gold, and silver, and with precious stones, and pleasant things.

Daniel 11:39 adds that this "strange god" will help the Antichrist defeat the strongest opponents during his rise to power:

> Thus shall he do in the most strong holds with a strange god, whom he shall acknowledge and increase with glory: and he shall cause them to rule over many, and shall divide the land for gain.

Daniel 8 also confirms that the Antichrist will receive outside help during his rise to power. He will receive immense power and will crush his enemies:

> Daniel 8:23-25
>
> (23) And in the latter time of their kingdom, when the transgressors are come to the full, a king of fierce countenance, and understanding dark sentences, shall stand up.
> (24) **And his power shall be mighty, but not by his own power:** and he shall destroy wonderfully, and shall prosper, and practise, and shall destroy the mighty and the holy people.
> (25) And through his policy also he shall cause craft to prosper in his hand; and he shall magnify himself in his heart, and by peace shall destroy many: he shall also stand up against the Prince of princes; but he shall be broken without hand.

We can use Revelation 13 to find the identity of the "god of forces". Revelation 13 tells us that the dragon will be the source of Antichrist's power during his reign. Interestingly, the people of the earth will worship the beast of Revelation 13 (through the worship of the Antichrist) *and the dragon*:

> Revelation 13:2-4
>
> (2) And the beast which I saw was like unto a leopard, and his

feet were as the feet of a bear, and his mouth as the mouth of a lion: and the dragon gave him his power, and his seat, and great authority.
(3) And I saw one of his heads as it were wounded to death; and his deadly wound was healed: and all the world wondered after the beast.
(4) And they worshipped the dragon which gave power unto the beast: and they worshipped the beast, saying, Who is like unto the beast? who is able to make war with him?

Revelation 12:9 tells us that the dragon represents Satan:

And the great dragon was cast out, that old serpent, called the Devil, and Satan, which deceiveth the whole world: he was cast out into the earth, and his angels were cast out with him.

Also, Revelation 13:2 tells us that the dragon will give the beast (through the Antichrist) "his power, and his seat, and great authority." Satan offered Christ the kingdoms of the earth and the glory that comes with being the ruler of the world if He would worship Satan (Matthew 4:8-9, Luke 4:5-7). Christ rejected Satan's offer and rebuked him for tempting Him. In contrast, Antichrist will accept Satan's offer. The Antichrist will acknowledge the dragon Satan and will compel the world to worship the dragon alongside him.

Given all this, the god of forces is most likely Satan since he will be the one who gives Antichrist his power. Thus, the Antichrist will likely honor Satan when he sets up the abomination of desolation.

This will take place when Satan unleashes his biggest end time deception. With the help of Satan, Antichrist will appear to the world as a man who has been resurrected from the dead. The world will marvel at the Antichrist and heed his calls to worship him and the dragon who gives him his power (Revelation 13:2-4).

The End Time Yom Kippur

Recall that the 70th week of Daniel or tribulation will last for 2,520 days. Its end is likely to take place on the Jewish holiday of Yom Kippur, the Day of Atonement. Yom Kippur is a solemn day where practitioners seek to repent of their sins and seek reconciliation with God.

The significance of Yom Kippur aligns with what will take place at the end of the 70th week of Daniel. Recall that several events will begin to come to pass at the end of the 70th week of Daniel, including:

- The atonement for the sins of Jerusalem and the people of Israel.
- Reconciliation for Israel's iniquity.

The Bible suggests that these events will begin to come to pass on the Day of Atonement at the end of the tribulation. The Book of Joel describes one of the solemn or sacred assemblies that will take place at that time.[1] The scene described is consistent with the observance of Yom Kippur (see Figure 1):

Figure 1: A Solemn Assembly on Yom Kippur?

- **Humble Oneself to the Lord**
- **A Sacred Assembly**

Leviticus 23:27-28

(27) Also on the tenth day of this seventh month there shall be a day of atonement: **it shall be an holy convocation unto you; and ye shall afflict your souls**, and offer an offering made by fire unto the Lord.
(28) And ye shall do no work in that same day: for it is a day of atonement, to make an atonement for you before the Lord your God.

Joel 1:13-15

(13) Gird yourselves, and lament, ye priests: howl, ye ministers of the altar: come, lie all night in sackcloth, ye ministers of my God: for the meat offering and the drink offering is withholden from the house of your God.
(14) **Sanctify ye a fast, call a solemn assembly**, gather the elders and all the inhabitants of the land into the house of the Lord your God, **and cry unto the Lord,**
(15) Alas for the day! for the day of the Lord is at hand, and as a destruction from the Almighty shall it come.

Joel 2:15-17

(15) Blow the trumpet in Zion, **sanctify a fast, call a solemn assembly:**
(16) Gather the people, sanctify the congregation, assemble the elders, gather the children, and those that suck the breasts: let the bridegroom go forth of his chamber, and the bride out of her closet.
(17) **Let the priests, the ministers of the Lord, weep between the porch and the altar, and let them say, Spare thy people, O Lord, and give not thine heritage to reproach, that the**

heathen should rule over them: wherefore should they say among the people, Where is their God?

Therefore, we can expect the end of the tribulation to occur on Yom Kippur. This detail will be important as we consider the timing of other key end time events.

The Jubilee Year

The Lord instructed the people of Israel to follow a 7-year agricultural cycle (Exodus 23:10-11, Leviticus 25:3-7). The people would work the land for the first 6 years of the cycle and not work the land during the 7th year. This 7th year would be a year of rest for the land or a Sabbath Year.

A Jubilee Year is a special Sabbath Year observed once every 50 years. This special year begins on the Day of Atonement or Yom Kippur. At that time, property must return to its original owner and people must be set free:

> Leviticus 25:9-10
>
> (9) Then shalt thou cause the trumpet of the jubile to sound on the tenth day of the seventh month, in the day of atonement shall ye make the trumpet sound throughout all your land.
> (10) And ye shall hallow the fiftieth year, **and proclaim liberty throughout all the land unto all the inhabitants** thereof: it shall be a jubile unto you; and **ye shall return every man unto his possession, and ye shall return every man unto his family.**

Isaiah 61:1-2, a passage about Christ's First Coming and Second Coming, indicates that the end of the tribulation may coincide with the start of a Jubilee Year. The passage mentions that the Lord will come to set people free:

Isaiah 61:1-2

(1) The Spirit of the Lord God is upon me; because the Lord hath anointed me to preach good tidings unto the meek; he hath sent me to bind up the brokenhearted, **to proclaim liberty to the captives, and the opening of the prison to them that are bound;**
(2) **To proclaim the acceptable year of the Lord,** and the day of vengeance of our God; to comfort all that mourn;

The details in Isaiah 61:1-2 mirror Leviticus 25:9-10 (see Figure 2). This strongly suggests that "the acceptable year of the Lord" is a Jubilee Year:

Figure 2: The End Time Jubilee Year

- **Proclaim Liberty**
- **The Return of People**

    Leviticus 25:9-10

    (9) Then shalt thou cause the trumpet of the jubile to sound on the tenth day of the seventh month, in the day of atonement shall ye make the trumpet sound throughout all your land.
    (10) And ye shall hallow the fiftieth year, **and proclaim liberty throughout all the land unto all the inhabitants** thereof: it shall be a jubile unto you; and ye shall return every man unto his possession, **and ye shall return every man unto his family.**

    Isaiah 61:1-2

    (1) The Spirit of the Lord God is upon me; because the Lord hath anointed me to preach good tidings unto the meek; he hath sent me to bind up the brokenhearted, **to proclaim liberty to the captives, and the opening of the prison to them that are bound;**
    (2) To proclaim the acceptable year of the Lord, and the day of vengeance of our God; to comfort all that mourn;

As stated in Leviticus 25:9-10, property returns to its original owner and people are set free in a Jubilee Year. The events described by Isaiah match what takes place in a Jubilee Year. The Lord will free the people of Israel from their captivity (Isaiah 61:1-2). He will also cause them to regain the land of their ancestors and prosper (Deuteronomy 30:5, Isaiah 61:3-5).

The Second Coming of Christ

Recall that Christ taught that the heavenly signs heralding His Second Coming would appear after the great tribulation ends:

> Matthew 24:29-31
>
> (29) Immediately after the tribulation of those days shall the sun be darkened, and the moon shall not give her light, and the stars shall fall from heaven, and the powers of the heavens shall be shaken:
> (30) And then shall appear the sign of the Son of man in heaven: and then shall all the tribes of the earth mourn, and they shall see the Son of man coming in the clouds of heaven with power and great glory.
> (31) And he shall send his angels with a great sound of a trumpet, and they shall gather together his elect from the four winds, from one end of heaven to the other.

We can glean from this that the Second Coming of Christ will take place shortly after the end of the great tribulation and end of the tribulation.[2] Isaiah 61:1-2 confirms this timing when it refers to the Second Coming of Christ at the onset of a Jubilee Year.

1290 & 1335 Days After the Midpoint

Daniel 12 mentions two periods that begin when the daily sacrifice stops at the midpoint of the 70th week. The first spans 1,290 days from the time the daily sacrifice stops to the removal of the abomination of desolation:

> Daniel 12:11
>
> And from the time that the daily sacrifice shall be taken away, and the abomination that maketh desolate set up, there shall be a thousand two hundred and ninety days.

We can glean that the abomination of desolation is likely to be in place for 1,290 days after the midpoint of the 70th week and its removal will occur 30-days after the end of the 70th week.

The second period spans 1,335 days from the time the daily sacrifice stops to a time when a living person will be blessed:

> Daniel 12:11-12
>
> (11) And from the time that the daily sacrifice shall be taken away, and the abomination that maketh desolate set up, there shall be a thousand two hundred and ninety days.
> (12) Blessed is he that waiteth, and cometh to the thousand three hundred and five and thirty days.

Although verse 12 is unclear about why someone who sees the 1,335th day will be blessed, we may deduce what may take place on the 1,335th day by considering the calendar.

Recall that the end of the 70th week of Daniel will occur 1,260 days after the daily sacrifice stops, coinciding with the Jewish holiday of Yom Kippur. Therefore, 75 days is the difference between the end of the 70th week of Daniel and the 1,335th day from the time the daily sacrifice stops. Amazingly, the Jewish holiday of Hanukkah falls approximately 75 days after Yom Kippur!

Hanukkah (Hebrew meaning "dedication") commemorates the rededication of the Second Temple that was purified after Antiochus Epiphanes IV desecrated it with an abomination of desolation in the 2nd century B.C. The potential significance of Hanukkah occurring at the end of this 75-day period is that it may herald the dedication or rededication of a temple from where the Lord will reign in the Millennium.

The dedication or rededication of a temple occurs when it is ready for use. This suggests that the Lord will be ready to rule the nations of the earth from it at the start of the Millennium. Therefore, we can conclude that the Millennium will likely commence after the 75-day period.

Figure 3 summarizes the events we have looked at in this chapter and past chapters in timeline form. Recall that "the tribulation" is a term to describe the 70th week of Daniel.

Figure 3: Outline of Events

Start of the Tribulation

- Confirmation of the 7-Year Covenant

Midpoint of the Tribulation (Day 1,260)

- The Daily Sacrifice Stops
- Abomination of Desolation is Set Up
- Antichrist Claims to be Resurrected
- The Great Tribulation Begins

End of the Tribulation (Day 2,520)

- Yom Kippur
- Start of a Jubilee Year
- The Heavenly Signs Appear
- The Second Coming of Christ

Abomination of Desolation Removal

- 1,290 Days Since the Midpoint

The Start of the Millennium Kingdom

- Hanukkah
- 1,335 Days Since the Midpoint

Let's Pause for a Moment

We looked at several key dates in this chapter. We learned that:

- The tribulation is likely to end on a future Yom Kippur.
- The end of the tribulation is likely to coincide with the start of a Jubilee Year.
- The Second Coming of Christ will take place shortly after the end of the tribulation. The heavenly signs will appear just before this event.
- Hanukkah is likely to herald the start of the Millennium approximately 75 days later.

Keep these details in mind because we will use them to answer whether we are the last generation before the coming of Christ.

Notes

1. How do we know that Joel pertains to the end of the tribulation? Joel 2:18 onward describes how the Lord will help His people after they seek Him. This response is the Second Coming of Christ.
2. I believe the end of the great tribulation and end of the tribulation will take place at the same time.

Daniel's 2,300-Day Prophecy

We will take what we learned in the last chapter to talk about one more end time timeline: Daniel's 2,300-day prophecy. We will look at this prophecy since some have tried to use it to predict when Christ will return.

The Daily Sacrifice

Recall that the daily sacrifice will take place in the 70th week of Daniel (Daniel 9:27). This will be a huge development since no daily sacrifice has taken place since the Romans destroyed the Second Temple in 70 A.D.

Although the Bible says nothing specific, the 7-year covenant with many could permit the building of the Third Temple and permit the daily sacrifice to start.[1] Daniel 8 may tell us when we will see the daily sacrifice start after the 70th week of Daniel begins.

Past & Future

Daniel 2,300-day prophecy is about the past and the future. Many believe the vision in Daniel 8:9-14 is about Antiochus Epiphanes IV:

> (9) And out of one of them came forth a little horn, which waxed exceeding great, toward the south, and toward the east, and toward the pleasant land.
> (10) And it waxed great, even to the host of heaven; and it cast down some of the host and of the stars to the ground, and stamped upon them.
> (11) Yea, he magnified himself even to the prince of the host,

and by him the daily sacrifice was taken away, and the place of the sanctuary was cast down.

(12) And an host was given him against the daily sacrifice by reason of transgression, and it cast down the truth to the ground; and it practised, and prospered.

(13) Then I heard one saint speaking, and another saint said unto that certain saint which spake, How long shall be the vision concerning the daily sacrifice, and the transgression of desolation, to give both the sanctuary and the host to be trodden under foot?

(14) And he said unto me, Unto two thousand and three hundred days; then shall the sanctuary be cleansed.

However, the vision is also about the end times. The Angel Gabriel told Daniel that the vision pertains to the time of the end:

Daniel 8:15-19

(15) And it came to pass, when I, even I Daniel, had seen the vision, and sought for the meaning, then, behold, there stood before me as the appearance of a man.

(16) And I heard a man's voice between the banks of Ulai, which called, and said, Gabriel, make this man to understand the vision.

(17) So he came near where I stood: and when he came, I was afraid, and fell upon my face: but he said unto me, Understand, O son of man: for at **the time of the end shall be the vision**.

(18) Now as he was speaking with me, I was in a deep sleep on my face toward the ground: but he touched me, and set me upright.

(19) And he said, Behold, I will make thee know what shall be in the last end of the indignation: for at the time appointed the end shall be.

Many believe Daniel 8:20-22 is about the period spanning from the rise of Alexander the Great to the division of his empire after his death. Daniel 8:23 onward is about the Antichrist in the end times:

> (23) And in the latter time of their kingdom, when the transgressors are come to the full, a king of fierce countenance, and understanding dark sentences, shall stand up.
> (24) And his power shall be mighty, but not by his own power: and he shall destroy wonderfully, and shall prosper, and practise, and shall destroy the mighty and the holy people.
> (25) And through his policy also he shall cause craft to prosper in his hand; and he shall magnify himself in his heart, and by peace shall destroy many: he shall also stand up against the Prince of princes; but he shall be broken without hand.
> (26) And the vision of the evening and the morning which was told is true: wherefore shut thou up the vision; for it shall be for many days.

The phrase "the vision of the evening and the morning" in verse 26 refers to the daily sacrifice and relates to a 2,300-day time frame of verse 14. Daniel 8:13-14 states that the 2,300 days pertain to:

- The daily sacrifice
- The abomination of desolation
- The cleansing of the sanctuary

The 2,300 Day Timeline

We can use this information to glean much about the daily sacrifice timeline. Let's look at the end date of the 2,300-day prophecy and work backwards to find its start:[2]

- We saw that the abomination of desolation will be in place for 1,290 days after the midpoint of the 70th week of Daniel or until the 2,550th day after the 70th week of Daniel starts (Daniel 12:11).
- Daniel 8:14 states that the cleansing of the temple will take place on the last day of the 2,300-day time frame. This means that the

end of the 2,300-day time frame will fall on the 2,550th day after the 70th week of Daniel starts.
- Subtracting 2,300 days from the 2,550th day means that the 2,300-day time frame will start on the 250th day after the 70th week of Daniel begins.
- The first day of the 2,300-day prophecy concerns the daily sacrifice, so we can deduce that the daily sacrifice will start on the 250th day of the 70th week of Daniel.

Figure 1 shows how the 2,300-day time frame fits into everything we have learned so far. Recall that "the tribulation" is a term to describe the 70th week of Daniel:

Figure 1: Outline of Events

Start of the Tribulation

- Confirmation of the 7-Year Covenant

The Daily Sacrifice Begins (Day 250)

- Start of the 2,300-Day Prophecy

Midpoint of the Tribulation (Day 1,260)

- The Daily Sacrifice Stops
- Abomination of Desolation is Set Up
- Antichrist Claims to be Resurrected
- The Great Tribulation Begins

End of the Tribulation (Day 2,520)

- Yom Kippur
- Start of a Jubilee Year
- The Heavenly Signs Appear
- The Second Coming of Christ

Abomination of Desolation Removal

- 1,290 Days Since the Midpoint
- The 2,300-Day Prophecy Ends

The Start of the Millennium Kingdom

- Hanukkah
- 1,335 Days Since the Midpoint

Let's Pause for a Moment

Daniel's 2,300-day prophecy helps us to learn when to expect the daily sacrifice to start in the tribulation. However, it is not a prophecy that I would use to pinpoint when Christ will return.

We will next look at plausible dates for the start and the end of the tribulation and the Second Coming of Christ.

Notes

1. It should not take long to erect a new temple once building is permitted. Several groups within Israel are ready to act as soon as building is allowed. These groups have also already made many of the items that will be part of the temple.
2. Some argue that the 2,300 days equates to 2,300 years. I do not believe this is the case in Daniel 8. Days are called "the evening and the morning" in Daniel 8. This term refers to:

    - The times of day when the sacrifice would take place.
    - The aspects of a calendar day.

    This leads me to believe that 2,300 days are 2,300 calendar days instead of years.

End Time Reckoning

Many enjoy the challenge of estimating when the tribulation will begin. I often get emails from people who offer their best guesses.

I was a teenager when I first tried to find when the tribulation would begin. I tried various methods and theories to come up with potential end time dates.

Ironically, I dislike the public practice of setting dates for the end of the world. This practice can give people false hopes and expectations. For instance,

- I have consoled people who experienced great anxiety and fear after a date setter gave them the sense that the world would soon end.
- I have also read about people who have lost friends and even their wealth after succumbing to the false predictions of date setters.

I do not want you to fall victim to the predictions of date setters. I will share with you plausible start dates and end dates for the tribulation and the Second Coming of Christ in this chapter. This information will help give you a good idea of which dates are possible and *not possible* for these events.

Can We Find the Jubilee Year?

Recall that the end of the tribulation is likely to coincide with the onset of a Jubilee Year. As a teenager, I thought we could identify when the tribulation will end and begin by finding the date of the next Jubilee Year. However, I quickly realized this is a huge challenge for these reasons:

- Debate exists about when the Israelites began to count Sabbath Years and Jubilee Years. Some argue they began to count as soon as they entered the land of Canaan. Others argue that they did not begin to count until after the conquest of Canaan.
- Debate exists about how to count the time span between Jubilee Years properly. Some believe we should count every 49 years. Others believe we should count every 50 years.
- The Jubilee Year has not been observed in a long time, so finding a reliable year from the past to anchor other calculations is not straightforward.
- Sabbath Years are observed today, but some doubt they are being observed on the correct years.

As you can see, calculating the possible start date and end date of the tribulation by finding the next Jubilee Year is not an ideal approach. Thankfully, I found a method that does not rely on the need to find a Jubilee Year or a Sabbath Year. I will share this method and my findings with you shortly.

A Word of Caution

Before we begin, we need to recognize that only God truly knows when the tribulation will begin and end and when Christ will come. We are finite creatures whose knowledge pales in comparison to God, and our knowledge of His plans is lacking:

> Isaiah 55:8-9
>
> (8) For my thoughts are not your thoughts, neither are your ways my ways, saith the Lord.
> (9) For as the heavens are higher than the earth, so are my ways higher than your ways, and my thoughts than your thoughts.

Furthermore, Christ said that only God knows the exact date and hour of His coming:

Matthew 24:36

> But of that day and hour knoweth no man, no, not the angels of heaven, but my Father only.

We can try to find which dates are possible for these events. But, it's unwise to claim that we can precisely know when these events will take place. We do not even know what tomorrow will bring in our lives:

James 4:13-15

> (13) Go to now, ye that say, To day or to morrow we will go into such a city, and continue there a year, and buy and sell, and get gain:
> (14) Whereas ye know not what shall be on the morrow. For what is your life? It is even a vapour, that appeareth for a little time, and then vanisheth away.
> (15) For that ye ought to say, If the Lord will, we shall live, and do this, or that.

We will identify which dates this century are possible through the process of elimination, but time will tell which of these dates are right (if any of them are right).

The Process of Elimination

We will start by looking at two key details. These details will help us eliminate many years and timelines from consideration.

Yom Kippur to Hanukkah

We learned in a previous chapter about a 75-day period that will follow the end of the 70th week of Daniel or on Yom Kippur.

Recall that I wrote that Hanukkah is *approximately* 75 days from

Yom Kippur. The reason I wrote this is that Hanukkah does not always fall 75 days after Yom Kippur. The following years *do not* have Yom Kippur and Hanukkah separated by 75 days:

- 2023, 2025, 2028, 2029
- 2031, 2032, 2035, 2036, 2038
- 2040, 2041, 2043, 2045, 2047, 2048
- 2051, 2052, 2055, 2056, 2058, 2059
- 2062, 2063, 2065, 2067, 2068
- 2070, 2072, 2074, 2075, 2078, 2079
- 2082, 2083, 2085, 2086, 2088
- 2090, 2092, 2094, 2095, 2098, 2099

I believe that the 75-day period alluded to in Daniel must span from Yom Kippur to Hanukkah since both holidays hold great end time significance. As a result, I do not believe these years can serve as end dates for the tribulation or serve as dates for the Second Coming of Christ.

When Satan's Biggest Deception Comes

Recall that the false resurrection of the Antichrist will be Satan's counterfeit attempt to make Antichrist seem like Jesus Christ. But Satan may go one step further to have Antichrist mimic what Christ did. Consider these facts:

- The Antichrist will claim that he's been resurrected from the dead at the midpoint of the tribulation.
- The second half of the tribulation will span 1,260 days and will end on the Jewish Holiday of Yom Kippur.

The reason I bring these facts up is that the midpoint of the tribulation may take place on Easter if it falls on certain years. In other words, the Antichrist could claim that he's been resurrected from the dead on the same day Christians celebrate the resurrection of Jesus Christ!

I acknowledge that the Bible does not state that the midpoint of the tribulation will fall on Easter. But, I believe it is very likely that the midpoint will fall on Easter since Satan will try to counterfeit Christ's resurrection.

The following tribulation timelines would have its midpoint fall on Easter: [1]

- 2026-2033 | 2033-2040 | 2040-2047
- 2043-2050 | 2046-2053 | 2053-2060
- 2060-2067 | 2063-2070 | 2067-2074
- 2070-2077 | 2073-2080 | 2087-2094
- 2090-2097 | 2091-2098

Some of these timelines have tribulation end dates that have already been cut. This means that we can eliminate many of the timelines listed here.

Surviving the Cut

We will next look at the timelines that remain for the rest of this century. Only 7 timelines remain. These timelines show plausible dates for the start and end of the tribulation and the Second Coming of Christ:

Figure 1: 2026-2033 Timeline

Start of the Tribulation

- November 8, 2026
- Confirmation of the 7-Year Covenant

The Daily Sacrifice Begins (Day 250)

- July 16, 2027
- Start of the 2,300-Day Prophecy

Midpoint of the Tribulation (Day 1,260)

- Easter Sunday: April 21, 2030
- The Daily Sacrifice Stops
- Abomination of Desolation is Set Up
- Antichrist Claims to be Resurrected
- The Great Tribulation Begins

End of the Tribulation (Day 2,520)

- Yom Kippur: October 2, 2033
- Start of a Jubilee Year
- The Heavenly Signs Appear
- The Second Coming of Christ

Abomination of Desolation Removal

- November 1, 2033
- 1,290 Days Since the Midpoint
- The 2,300-Day Prophecy Ends

Start of the Millennium Kingdom

- Hanukkah: December 16, 2033
- 1,335 Days Since the Midpoint

Figure 2: 2043-2050 Timeline

Start of the Tribulation

- November 1, 2043
- Confirmation of the 7-Year Covenant

The Daily Sacrifice Begins (Day 250)

- July 8, 2044
- Start of the 2,300-Day Prophecy

Midpoint of the Tribulation (Day 1,260)

- Easter Sunday: April 14, 2047
- The Daily Sacrifice Stops
- Abomination of Desolation is Set Up
- Antichrist Claims to be Resurrected
- The Great Tribulation Begins

End of the Tribulation (Day 2,520)

- Yom Kippur: September 25, 2050
- Start of a Jubilee Year
- The Heavenly Signs Appear
- The Second Coming of Christ

Abomination of Desolation Removal

- October 25, 2050
- 1,290 Days Since the Midpoint
- The 2,300-Day Prophecy Ends

Start of the Millennium Kingdom

- Hanukkah: December 9, 2050
- 1,335 Days Since the Midpoint

Figure 3: 2046-2053 Timeline

Start of the Tribulation

- October 28, 2046
- Confirmation of the 7-Year Covenant

The Daily Sacrifice Begins (Day 250)

- July 5, 2047
- Start of the 2,300-Day Prophecy

Midpoint of the Tribulation (Day 1,260)

- Easter Sunday: April 10, 2050
- The Daily Sacrifice Stops
- Abomination of Desolation is Set Up
- Antichrist Claims to be Resurrected
- The Great Tribulation Begins

End of the Tribulation (Day 2,520)

- Yom Kippur: September 21, 2053
- Start of a Jubilee Year
- The Heavenly Signs Appear
- The Second Coming of Christ

Abomination of Desolation Removal

- October 21, 2053
- 1,290 Days Since the Midpoint
- The 2,300-Day Prophecy Ends

Start of the Millennium Kingdom

- Hanukkah: December 5, 2053
- 1,335 Days Since the Midpoint

Figure 4: 2053-2060 Timeline

Start of the Tribulation

- November 9, 2053
- Confirmation of the 7-Year Covenant

The Daily Sacrifice Begins (Day 250)

- July 17, 2054
- Start of the 2,300-Day Prophecy

Midpoint of the Tribulation (Day 1,260)

- Easter Sunday: April 22, 2057
- The Daily Sacrifice Stops
- Abomination of Desolation is Set Up
- Antichrist Claims to be Resurrected
- The Great Tribulation Begins

End of the Tribulation (Day 2,520)

- Yom Kippur: October 3, 2060
- Start of a Jubilee Year
- The Heavenly Signs Appear
- The Second Coming of Christ

Abomination of Desolation Removal

- November 2, 2060
- 1,290 Days Since the Midpoint
- The 2,300-Day Prophecy Ends

Start of the Millennium Kingdom

- Hanukkah: December 17, 2060
- 1,335 Days Since the Midpoint

Figure 5: 2070-2077 Timeline

Start of the Tribulation

- November 2, 2070
- Confirmation of the 7-Year Covenant

The Daily Sacrifice Begins (Day 250)

- July 10, 2071
- Start of the 2,300-Day Prophecy

Midpoint of the Tribulation (Day 1,260)

- Easter Sunday: April 15, 2074
- The Daily Sacrifice Stops
- Abomination of Desolation is Set Up
- Antichrist Claims to be Resurrected
- The Great Tribulation Begins

End of the Tribulation (Day 2,520)

- Yom Kippur: September 26, 2077
- Start of a Jubilee Year
- The Heavenly Signs Appear
- The Second Coming of Christ

Abomination of Desolation Removal

- October 26, 2077
- 1,290 Days Since the Midpoint
- The 2,300-Day Prophecy Ends

Start of the Millennium Kingdom

- Hanukkah: December 10, 2077
- 1,335 Days Since the Midpoint

Figure 6: 2073-2080 Timeline

Start of the Tribulation

- October 29, 2073
- Confirmation of the 7-Year Covenant

The Daily Sacrifice Begins (Day 250)

- July 6, 2074
- Start of the 2,300-Day Prophecy

Midpoint of the Tribulation (Day 1,260)

- Easter Sunday: April 11, 2077
- The Daily Sacrifice Stops
- Abomination of Desolation is Set Up
- Antichrist Claims to be Resurrected
- The Great Tribulation Begins

End of the Tribulation (Day 2,520)

- Yom Kippur: September 22, 2080
- Start of a Jubilee Year
- The Heavenly Signs Appear
- The Second Coming of Christ

Abomination of Desolation Removal

- October 22, 2080
- 1,290 Days Since the Midpoint
- The 2,300-Day Prophecy Ends

Start of the Millennium Kingdom

- Hanukkah: December 6, 2080
- 1,335 Days Since the Midpoint

Figure 7: 2090-2097 Timeline

Start of the Tribulation

- October 22, 2090
- Confirmation of the 7-Year Covenant

The Daily Sacrifice Begins (Day 250)

- June 29, 2091
- Start of the 2,300-Day Prophecy

Midpoint of the Tribulation (Day 1,260)

- Easter Sunday: April 4, 2094
- The Daily Sacrifice Stops
- Abomination of Desolation is Set Up
- Antichrist Claims to be Resurrected
- The Great Tribulation Begins

End of the Tribulation (Day 2,520)

- Yom Kippur: September 15, 2097
- Start of a Jubilee Year
- The Heavenly Signs Appear
- The Second Coming of Christ

Abomination of Desolation Removal

- October 15, 2097
- 1,290 Days Since the Midpoint
- The 2,300-Day Prophecy Ends

Start of the Millennium Kingdom

- Hanukkah: November 29, 2097
- 1,335 Days Since the Midpoint

The earliest that the tribulation could begin according to these calculations is in 2026. For a 2026 start date to be possible, global conditions would have to get much worse in the next few years. We would see the world become so chaotic in a brief span of time that many would soon seek someone like the Antichrist to bring order to it.

The 2043 to 2050 timeline is not too far away from our present time. We would likely see worsening global conditions as we approach the year 2043, but not at the same pace we would see if 2026 served as the start of the tribulation.

With all the chaos now, it may be hard to see how the tribulation can start after 2053. However, the world would likely see more great leaps in technology by that time. These advances could boost the Antichrist's ability to control and kill people during the great tribulation.

Tribulation Season

I want to draw special attention to the start dates of each timeline. The start dates range from late October to early November. This means that we should mainly focus on late October to early November in each year we are looking for the start of the tribulation.

Recall that the tribulation or the 70th week of Daniel will start with the confirmation of a 7-year covenant with many.[2] We should expect this event to take place in late October or early November in the year the tribulation begins.

Are We the Last Generation?

We began this book asking: "Are we the last generation before the coming of Christ?" My answer to that question after researching the issue is "*Perhaps we are*".

The earliest plausible timeline identified in this study suggests we could see the tribulation begin as soon as 2026. If the tribulation starts in 2026, it will occur less than 80 years after the creation of the state of Israel in 1948. This start date would be within the 70 to 80-year generation time span offered in Psalm 90:10.

However, remember that the Parable of the Fig Tree is not about the creation of the state of Israel in 1948. The parable is about the heavenly signs that will appear just before the coming of Christ. Therefore, I would not identify 2026 as the likeliest date for the start of the tribulation just because it falls less than 80 years after 1948.

A 2033 Second Coming Theory

You will likely hear a lot of talk about how the Second Coming of Christ may take place in 2033. This talk centers on Hosea 6:1-2. The passage focuses on Israel's return to the Lord's care:

> (1) Come, and let us return unto the Lord: for he hath torn, and he will heal us; he hath smitten, and he will bind us up.
> (2) After two days will he revive us: in the third day he will raise us up, and we shall live in his sight.

Hosea 6:1-2 describes the Lord acting "after two days" and on the "third day". Some believe each day represents 1,000 years based on Psalm 90:4 and 2 Peter 3:8. You may hear some argue that:

- "Two days" (2,000 years) refers to Christ's Second Coming when He will restore Israel.
- The "third day" refers to Israel in the Millennium.

We saw that Christ was crucified in 33 A.D. The year 2033 would be 2,000 years from the time of His crucifixion. The theory is that

Christ will return to restore Israel in 2033 after "two days". The theory places the tribulation from 2026 to 2033.

I cannot endorse this theory because I am not a fan of equating 1 day to 1,000 years. The Bible compares a day to the Lord to 1,000 years in Psalm 90:4 and 2 Peter 3:8. But it does not state that a day is equal to 1,000 years:

> Psalm 90:4
> For a thousand years in thy sight are but as yesterday when it is past, and as a watch in the night.

> 2 Peter 3:8
> But, beloved, be not ignorant of this one thing, that one day is with the Lord as a thousand years, and a thousand years as one day.

I believe these verses are just trying to tell us that God's sense of timing differs from our own.

Nevertheless, I cannot rule out 2033 as the year for Christ's Second Coming yet. The 2026 to 2033 timeline is feasible. The theory may prove to be correct (or incorrect).

Other Thoughts

Could we see the tribulation begin in 2043 or 2046? We might, but we will have to see global conditions become much worse than they are now (as of 2020) soon. However, it is not unimaginable for global conditions to deteriorate rapidly since the coronavirus pandemic has shown us how quickly the world can change in a short amount of time.

The later plausible timelines (2053-2060, 2070-2077, 2073-2080, and 2090-2097) imply that we are not living in the last generation before the coming of Christ. Many of you who are reading this book will not live long enough to see the events of the tribulation if any of these timelines comes to fruition. Given how bad living conditions are likely to be around the tribulation, not being alive at that time may not be such a bad thing.

Notes

1. I subtracted 1,260 days from Yom Kippur of each year to find the midpoint of the tribulation. I performed all date calculations and got dates of holidays at timeanddate.com. I account for the fact that Jewish dates begin at sundown. As a result, the dates for Yom Kippur and Hanukkah shown in this book are one day earlier than on timeanddate.com. For instance, the website lists Yom Kippur on October 3, 2033. However, Yom Kippur will start on October 2 at sundown and continue until sundown on October 3.
2. I believe the covenant with many is a peace treaty that will pertain to Israel and its neighbors.

A Final Word

As I stated, I do not want you to fall victim to the predictions of date setters. By considering the timelines presented in this book, you now have a strong sense of which dates are possible and *which dates are not possible* for the tribulation and the Second Coming of Christ.

For instance, a person promoting a 2022 to 2029 tribulation timeline might gain a large audience because they talk about a date that is near. You know that the tribulation is unlikely to begin in 2022 because:

- There is only a 74-day time span between Yom Kippur and Hanukkah in 2029.
- The 2026 tribulation midpoint will not occur on an Easter Sunday.

With this knowledge, you can tell people you know to not believe the teachings of the date setter and to not fall for the hype.

Remember, we cannot know the ways of God. Only God knows the exact date when the tribulation will begin and when the Second Coming of Christ will take place. As we wait for the start of the tribulation, we will need to keep abreast of events.

Keep studying Bible prophecy. Keep watch. One day the tribulation will arrive. You might see it arrive in your lifetime.

Insights on the End Times

I want to briefly tell you about *Prophecy Proof Insights on the End Times* because it is a resource I believe can help you learn more about Bible prophecy.

My book *Prophecy Proof Insights on the End Times* contains:

- 25 chapters to give you a full understanding of the end times and its difficulties.
- Thousands of Bible prophecy-related verses cited.
- 5 bonus studies on topics like the Gog-Magog invasion and Babylon's identity.
- An exhaustive Scripture index so you can use the book as a study guide.
- Timelines to help you easily keep track of end time events as you read.

To learn more, visit: www.prophecyproof.org/book/

Year By Year Timelines

I present my calculations for timelines thru the year 2099 in this section.[1] A feasible timeline has:

1. Yom Kippur to Hanukkah spanning 75 days
2. The tribulation midpoint coinciding with Easter

A timeline's feasibility is indicated in the title by "Yes" or "No".

2020-2027 Timeline: No

- T. Start: November 15, 2020
- D. Sacrifice Start: July 23, 2021
- T. Midpoint: April 28 2024
- Easter: March 31, 2024
- Yom Kippur: October 10, 2027
- Removal of AofD: November 9, 2027
- Hanukkah: December 24, 2027
- Yom Kippur to Hanukkah: 75 Days

2021-2028 Timeline: No

- T. Start: November 5, 2021
- D. Sacrifice Start: July 13, 2022
- T. Midpoint: April 18, 2025
- Easter: April 20, 2025
- Yom Kippur: September 29, 2028
- Removal of AofD: October 29, 2028
- Hanukkah: December 12, 2028
- Yom Kippur to Hanukkah: 74 Days

2022-2029 Timeline: No

- T. Start: October 25, 2022
- D. Sacrifice Start: July 2, 2023
- T. Midpoint: April 7, 2026
- Easter: April 5, 2026
- Yom Kippur: September 18, 2029
- Removal of AofD: October 18, 2029
- Hanukkah: December 1, 2029
- Yom Kippur to Hanukkah: 74 Days

2023-2030 Timeline: No

- T. Start: November 12, 2023
- D. Sacrifice Start: July 19, 2024
- T. Midpoint: April 25, 2027
- Easter: March 28, 2027
- Yom Kippur: October 6, 2030
- Removal of AofD: November 5, 2030
- Hanukkah: December 20, 2030
- Yom Kippur to Hanukkah: 75 Days

2024-2031 Timeline: No

- T. Start: November 1, 2024
- D. Sacrifice Start: July 9, 2025
- T. Midpoint: April 14, 2028
- Easter: April 16, 2028
- Yom Kippur: September 26, 2031
- Removal of AofD: October 26, 2031
- Hanukkah: December 9, 2031
- Yom Kippur to Hanukkah: 74 Days

2025-2032 Timeline: No

- T. Start: October 21, 2025
- D. Sacrifice Start: June 28, 2026
- T. Midpoint: April 3, 2029
- Easter: April 1, 2029
- Yom Kippur: September 14, 2032
- Removal of AofD: October 14, 2032
- Hanukkah: November 27, 2032
- Yom Kippur to Hanukkah: 74 Days

2026-2033 Timeline: Yes

- T. Start: November 8, 2026
- D. Sacrifice Start: July 16, 2027
- T. Midpoint: April 21, 2030
- Easter: April 21, 2030
- Yom Kippur: October 2, 2033
- Removal of AofD: November 1, 2033
- Hanukkah: December 16, 2033
- Yom Kippur to Hanukkah: 75 Days

2027-2034 Timeline: No

- T. Start: October 29, 2027
- D. Sacrifice Start: July 5, 2028
- T. Midpoint: April 11, 2031
- Easter: April 13, 2031
- Yom Kippur: September 22, 2034
- Removal of AofD: October 22, 2034
- Hanukkah: December 6, 2034
- Yom Kippur to Hanukkah: 75 Days

2028-2035 Timeline: No

- T. Start: November 17, 2028
- D. Sacrifice Start: July 25, 2029
- T. Midpoint: April 30, 2032
- Easter: March 28, 2032
- Yom Kippur: October 12, 2035
- Removal of AofD: November 11, 2035
- Hanukkah: December 25, 2035
- Yom Kippur to Hanukkah: 74 Days

2029-2036 Timeline: No

- T. Start: November 6, 2029
- D. Sacrifice Start: July 14, 2030
- T. Midpoint: April 19, 2033
- Easter: April 17, 2033
- Yom Kippur: September 30, 2036
- Removal of AofD: October 30, 2036
- Hanukkah: December 13, 2036
- Yom Kippur to Hanukkah: 74 Days

2030-2037 Timeline: No

- T. Start: October 25, 2030
- D. Sacrifice Start: July 2, 2031
- T. Midpoint: April 7, 2034
- Easter: April 9, 2034
- Yom Kippur: September 18, 2037
- Removal of AofD: October 18, 2037
- Hanukkah: December 2, 2037
- Yom Kippur to Hanukkah: 75 Days

2031-2038 Timeline: No

- T. Start: November 14, 2031
- D. Sacrifice Start: July 21, 2032
- T. Midpoint: April 27 2035
- Easter: March 25, 2035
- Yom Kippur: October 8, 2038
- Removal of AofD: November 7, 2038
- Hanukkah: December 21, 2038
- Yom Kippur to Hanukkah: 74 Days

2032-2039 Timeline: No

- T. Start: November 2, 2032
- D. Sacrifice Start: July 10, 2033
- T. Midpoint: April 15, 2036
- Easter: April 13, 2036
- Yom Kippur: September 27, 2039
- Removal of AofD: October 27, 2039
- Hanukkah: December 11, 2039
- Yom Kippur to Hanukkah: 75 Days

2033-2040 Timeline: No

- T. Start: October 23, 2033
- D. Sacrifice Start: June 30, 2034
- T. Midpoint: April 5, 2037
- Easter: April 5, 2037
- Yom Kippur: September 16, 2040
- Removal of AofD: October 16, 2040
- Hanukkah: November 29, 2040
- Yom Kippur to Hanukkah: 74 Days

2034-2041 Timeline: No

- T. Start: November 10, 2034
- D. Sacrifice Start: July 18, 2035
- T. Midpoint: April 23, 2038
- Easter: April 25, 2038
- Yom Kippur: October 4, 2041
- Removal of AofD: November 3, 2041
- Hanukkah: December 17, 2041
- Yom Kippur to Hanukkah: 74 Days

2035-2042 Timeline: No

- T. Start: October 30, 2035
- D. Sacrifice Start: July 6, 2036
- T. Midpoint: April 12, 2039
- Easter: April 10, 2039
- Yom Kippur: September 23, 2042
- Removal of AofD: October 23, 2042
- Hanukkah: December 7, 2042
- Yom Kippur to Hanukkah: 75 Days

2036-2043 Timeline: No

- T. Start: November 18, 2036
- D. Sacrifice Start: July 26, 2037
- T. Midpoint: May 1, 2040
- Easter: April 1, 2040
- Yom Kippur: October 13, 2043
- Removal of AofD: November 12, 2043
- Hanukkah: December 26, 2043
- Yom Kippur to Hanukkah: 74 Days

2037-2044 Timeline: No

- T. Start: November 6, 2037
- D. Sacrifice Start: July 14, 2038
- T. Midpoint: April 19, 2041
- Easter: April 21, 2041
- Yom Kippur: September 30, 2044
- Removal of AofD: October 30, 2044
- Hanukkah: December 14, 2044
- Yom Kippur to Hanukkah: 75 Days

2038-2045 Timeline: No

- T. Start: October 27, 2038
- D. Sacrifice Start: July 4, 2039
- T. Midpoint: April 9, 2042
- Easter: April 6, 2042
- Yom Kippur: September 20, 2045
- Removal of AofD: October 20, 2045
- Hanukkah: December 3, 2045
- Yom Kippur to Hanukkah: 74 Days

2039-2046 Timeline: No

- T. Start: November 15, 2039
- D. Sacrifice Start: July 22, 2040
- T. Midpoint: April 28, 2043
- Easter: March 29, 2043
- Yom Kippur: October 9, 2046
- Removal of AofD: November 8, 2046
- Hanukkah: December 23, 2046
- Yom Kippur to Hanukkah: 75 Days

2040-2047 Timeline: No

- T. Start: November 4, 2040
- D. Sacrifice Start: July 12, 2041
- T. Midpoint: April 17, 2044
- Easter: April 17, 2044
- Yom Kippur: September 29, 2047
- Removal of AofD: October 29, 2047
- Hanukkah: December 12, 2047
- Yom Kippur to Hanukkah: 74 Days

2041-2048 Timeline: No

- T. Start: October 23, 2041
- D. Sacrifice Start: June 30, 2042
- T. Midpoint: April 5, 2045
- Easter: April 9, 2045
- Yom Kippur: September 16, 2048
- Removal of AofD: October 16, 2048
- Hanukkah: November 29, 2048
- Yom Kippur to Hanukkah: 74 Days

2042-2049 Timeline: No

- T. Start: November 11, 2042
- D. Sacrifice Start: July 19, 2043
- T. Midpoint: April 24, 2046
- Easter: March 25, 2046
- Yom Kippur: October 5, 2049
- Removal of AofD: November 4, 2049
- Hanukkah: December 19, 2049
- Yom Kippur to Hanukkah: 75 Days

2043-2050 Timeline: Yes

- T. Start: November 1, 2043
- D. Sacrifice Start: July 8, 2044
- T. Midpoint: April 14, 2047
- Easter: April 14, 2047
- Yom Kippur: September 25, 2050
- Removal of AofD: October 25, 2050
- Hanukkah: December 9, 2050
- Yom Kippur to Hanukkah: 75 Days

2044-2051 Timeline: No

- T. Start: October 21, 2044
- D. Sacrifice Start: June 28, 2045
- T. Midpoint: April 3, 2048
- Easter: April 5, 2048
- Yom Kippur: September 15, 2051
- Removal of AofD: October 15, 2051
- Hanukkah: November 28, 2051
- Yom Kippur to Hanukkah: 74 Days

2045-2052 Timeline: No

- T. Start: November 8, 2045
- D. Sacrifice Start: July 16, 2046
- T. Midpoint: April 21, 2049
- Easter: April 18, 2049
- Yom Kippur: October 2, 2052
- Removal of AofD: November 1, 2052
- Hanukkah: December 15, 2052
- Yom Kippur to Hanukkah: 74 Days

2046-2053 Timeline: Yes

- T. Start: October 28, 2046
- D. Sacrifice Start: July 5, 2047
- T. Midpoint: April 10, 2050
- Easter: April 10, 2050
- Yom Kippur: September 21, 2053
- Removal of AofD: October 21, 2053
- Hanukkah: December 5, 2053
- Yom Kippur to Hanukkah: 75 Days

2047-2054 Timeline: No

- T. Start: November 17, 2047
- D. Sacrifice Start: July 24, 2048
- T. Midpoint: April 30, 2051
- Easter: April 2, 2051
- Yom Kippur: October 11, 2054
- Removal of AofD: November 10, 2054
- Hanukkah: December 25, 2054
- Yom Kippur to Hanukkah: 75 Days

2048-2055 Timeline: No

- T. Start: November 6, 2048
- D. Sacrifice Start: July 14, 2049
- T. Midpoint: April 19, 2052
- Easter: April 21, 2052
- Yom Kippur: October 1, 2055
- Removal of AofD: October 31, 2055
- Hanukkah: December 14, 2055
- Yom Kippur to Hanukkah: 74 Days

2049-2056 Timeline: No

- T. Start: October 26, 2049
- D. Sacrifice Start: July 3, 2050
- T. Midpoint: April 8, 2053
- Easter: April 6, 2053
- Yom Kippur: September 19, 2056
- Removal of AofD: October 19, 2056
- Hanukkah: December 2, 2056
- Yom Kippur to Hanukkah: 74 Days

2050-2057 Timeline: No

- T. Start: November 13, 2050
- D. Sacrifice Start: July 21, 2051
- T. Midpoint: April 26, 2054
- Easter: March 29, 2054
- Yom Kippur: October 7, 2057
- Removal of AofD: November 6, 2057
- Hanukkah: December 21, 2057
- Yom Kippur to Hanukkah: 75 Days

2051-2058 Timeline: No

- T. Start: November 3, 2051
- D. Sacrifice Start: July 10, 2052
- T. Midpoint: April 16, 2055
- Easter: April 18, 2055
- Yom Kippur: September 27, 2058
- Removal of AofD: October 27, 2058
- Hanukkah: December 10, 2058
- Yom Kippur to Hanukkah: 74 Days

2052-2059 Timeline: No

- T. Start: October 22, 2052
- D. Sacrifice Start: June 29, 2053
- T. Midpoint: April 4, 2056
- Easter: April 2, 2056
- Yom Kippur: September 16, 2059
- Removal of AofD: October 16, 2059
- Hanukkah: November 29, 2059
- Yom Kippur to Hanukkah: 74 Days

2053-2060 Timeline: Yes

- T. Start: November 9, 2053
- D. Sacrifice Start: July 17, 2054
- T. Midpoint: April 22, 2057
- Easter: April 22, 2057
- Yom Kippur: October 3, 2060
- Removal of AofD: November 2, 2060
- Hanukkah: December 17, 2060
- Yom Kippur to Hanukkah: 75 Days

2054-2061 Timeline: No

- T. Start: October 30, 2054
- D. Sacrifice Start: July 7, 2055
- T. Midpoint: April 12, 2058
- Easter: April 14, 2058
- Yom Kippur: September 23, 2061
- Removal of AofD: October 23, 2061
- Hanukkah: December 7, 2061
- Yom Kippur to Hanukkah: 75 Days

2055-2062 Timeline: No

- T. Start: November 19, 2055
- D. Sacrifice Start: July 26, 2056
- T. Midpoint: May 2, 2059
- Easter: March 30, 2059
- Yom Kippur: October 13, 2062
- Removal of AofD: November 12, 2062
- Hanukkah: December 26, 2062
- Yom Kippur to Hanukkah: 74 Days

2056-2063 Timeline: No

- T. Start: November 7, 2056
- D. Sacrifice Start: July 15, 2057
- T. Midpoint: April 20, 2060
- Easter: April 18, 2060
- Yom Kippur: October 2, 2063
- Removal of AofD: November 1, 2063
- Hanukkah: December 15, 2063
- Yom Kippur to Hanukkah: 74 Days

2057-2064 Timeline: No

- T. Start: October 26, 2057
- D. Sacrifice Start: July 3, 2058
- T. Midpoint: April 8, 2061
- Easter: April 10, 2061
- Yom Kippur: September 19, 2064
- Removal of AofD: October 19, 2064
- Hanukkah: December 3, 2064
- Yom Kippur to Hanukkah: 75 Days

2058-2065 Timeline: No

- T. Start: November 15, 2058
- D. Sacrifice Start: July 23, 2059
- T. Midpoint: April 28, 2062
- Easter: March 26, 2062
- Yom Kippur: October 9, 2065
- Removal of AofD: November 8, 2065
- Hanukkah: December 22, 2065
- Yom Kippur to Hanukkah: 74 Days

2059-2066 Timeline: No

- T. Start: November 4, 2059
- D. Sacrifice Start: July 11, 2060
- T. Midpoint: April 17, 2063
- Easter: April 15, 2063
- Yom Kippur: September 28, 2066
- Removal of AofD: October 28, 2066
- Hanukkah: December 12, 2066
- Yom Kippur to Hanukkah: 75 Days

2060-2067 Timeline: No

- T. Start: October 24, 2060
- D. Sacrifice Start: July 1, 2061
- T. Midpoint: April 6, 2064
- Easter: April 6, 2064
- Yom Kippur: September 18, 2067
- Removal of AofD: October 18, 2067
- Hanukkah: December 1, 2067
- Yom Kippur to Hanukkah: 74 Days

2061-2068 Timeline: No

- T. Start: November 11, 2061
- D. Sacrifice Start: July 19, 2062
- T. Midpoint: April 24, 2065
- Easter: March 29, 2065
- Yom Kippur: October 5, 2068
- Removal of AofD: November 4, 2068
- Hanukkah: December 18, 2068
- Yom Kippur to Hanukkah: 74 Days

2062-2069 Timeline: No

- T. Start: October 31, 2062
- D. Sacrifice Start: July 8, 2063
- T. Midpoint: April 13, 2066
- Easter: April 11, 2066
- Yom Kippur: September 24, 2069
- Removal of AofD: October 24, 2069
- Hanukkah: December 8, 2069
- Yom Kippur to Hanukkah: 75 Days

2063-2070 Timeline: No

- T. Start: October 21, 2063
- D. Sacrifice Start: June 27, 2064
- T. Midpoint: April 3, 2067
- Easter: April 3, 2067
- Yom Kippur: September 14, 2070
- Removal of AofD: October 14, 2070
- Hanukkah: November 27, 2070
- Yom Kippur to Hanukkah: 74 Days

2064-2071 Timeline: No

- T. Start: November 7, 2064
- D. Sacrifice Start: July 15, 2065
- T. Midpoint: April 20, 2068
- Easter: April 22, 2068
- Yom Kippur: October 2, 2071
- Removal of AofD: November 1, 2071
- Hanukkah: December 16, 2071
- Yom Kippur to Hanukkah: 75 Days

2065-2072 Timeline: No

- T. Start: October 28, 2065
- D. Sacrifice Start: July 5, 2066
- T. Midpoint: April 10, 2069
- Easter: April 14, 2069
- Yom Kippur: September 21, 2072
- Removal of AofD: October 21, 2072
- Hanukkah: December 4, 2072
- Yom Kippur to Hanukkah: 74 Days

2066-2073 Timeline: No

- T. Start: November 16, 2066
- D. Sacrifice Start: July 24, 2067
- T. Midpoint: April 29, 2070
- Easter: March 30, 2070
- Yom Kippur: October 10, 2073
- Removal of AofD: November 9, 2073
- Hanukkah: December 24, 2073
- Yom Kippur to Hanukkah: 75 Days

2067-2074 Timeline: No

- T. Start: November 6, 2067
- D. Sacrifice Start: July 13, 2068
- T. Midpoint: April 19, 2071
- Easter: April 19, 2071
- Yom Kippur: September 30, 2074
- Removal of AofD: October 30, 2074
- Hanukkah: December 13, 2074
- Yom Kippur to Hanukkah: 74 Days

2068-2075 Timeline: No

- T. Start: October 24, 2068
- D. Sacrifice Start: July 1, 2069
- T. Midpoint: April 6, 2072
- Easter: April 10, 2072
- Yom Kippur: September 18, 2075
- Removal of AofD: October 18, 2075
- Hanukkah: December 1, 2075
- Yom Kippur to Hanukkah: 74 Days

2069-2076 Timeline: No

- T. Start: November 12, 2069
- D. Sacrifice Start: July 20, 2070
- T. Midpoint: April 25, 2073
- Easter: March 26, 2073
- Yom Kippur: October 6, 2076
- Removal of AofD: November 5, 2076
- Hanukkah: December 20, 2076
- Yom Kippur to Hanukkah: 75 Days

2070-2077 Timeline: Yes

- T. Start: November 2, 2070
- D. Sacrifice Start: July 10, 2071
- T. Midpoint: April 15, 2074
- Easter: April 15, 2074
- Yom Kippur: September 26, 2077
- Removal of AofD: October 26, 2077
- Hanukkah: December 10, 2077
- Yom Kippur to Hanukkah: 75 Days

2071-2078 Timeline: No

- T. Start: October 23, 2071
- D. Sacrifice Start: June 29, 2072
- T. Midpoint: April 5, 2075
- Easter: April 7, 2075
- Yom Kippur: September 16, 2078
- Removal of AofD: October 16, 2078
- Hanukkah: November 29, 2078
- Yom Kippur to Hanukkah: 74 Days

2072-2079 Timeline: No

- T. Start: November 9, 2072
- D. Sacrifice Start: July 17, 2073
- T. Midpoint: April 22, 2076
- Easter: April 19, 2076
- Yom Kippur: October 4, 2079
- Removal of AofD: November 3, 2079
- Hanukkah: December 17, 2079
- Yom Kippur to Hanukkah: 74 Days

2073-2080 Timeline: Yes

- T. Start: October 29, 2073
- D. Sacrifice Start: July 6, 2074
- T. Midpoint: April 11, 2077
- Easter: April 11, 2077
- Yom Kippur: September 22, 2080
- Removal of AofD: October 22, 2080
- Hanukkah: December 6, 2080
- Yom Kippur to Hanukkah: 75 Days

2074-2081 Timeline: No

- T. Start: November 18, 2074
- D. Sacrifice Start: July 26, 2075
- T. Midpoint: May 1, 2078
- Easter: April 3, 2078
- Yom Kippur: October 12, 2081
- Removal of AofD: November 11, 2081
- Hanukkah: December 26, 2081
- Yom Kippur to Hanukkah: 75 Days

2075-2082 Timeline: No

- T. Start: November 8, 2075
- D. Sacrifice Start: July 15, 2076
- T. Midpoint: April 21, 2079
- Easter: April 16, 2079
- Yom Kippur: October 2, 2082
- Removal of AofD: November 1, 2082
- Hanukkah: December 15, 2082
- Yom Kippur to Hanukkah: 74 Days

2076-2083 Timeline: No

- T. Start: October 27, 2076
- D. Sacrifice Start: July 4, 2077
- T. Midpoint: April 9, 2080
- Easter: April 7, 2080
- Yom Kippur: September 21, 2083
- Removal of AofD: October 21, 2083
- Hanukkah: December 4, 2083
- Yom Kippur to Hanukkah: 74 Days

2077-2084 Timeline: No

- T. Start: November 14, 2077
- D. Sacrifice Start: July 22, 2078
- T. Midpoint: April 27, 2081
- Easter: March 30, 2081
- Yom Kippur: October 8, 2084
- Removal of AofD: November 7, 2084
- Hanukkah: December 22, 2084
- Yom Kippur to Hanukkah: 75 Days

2078-2085 Timeline: No

- T. Start: November 4, 2078
- D. Sacrifice Start: July 12, 2079
- T. Midpoint: April 17, 2082
- Easter: April 19, 2082
- Yom Kippur: September 28, 2085
- Removal of AofD: October 28, 2085
- Hanukkah: December 11, 2085
- Yom Kippur to Hanukkah: 74 Days

2079-2086 Timeline: No

- T. Start: October 24, 2079
- D. Sacrifice Start: June 30, 2080
- T. Midpoint: April 6, 2083
- Easter: April 4, 2083
- Yom Kippur: September 17, 2086
- Removal of AofD: October 17, 2086
- Hanukkah: November 30, 2086
- Yom Kippur to Hanukkah: 74 Days

2080-2087 Timeline: No

- T. Start: November 10, 2080
- D. Sacrifice Start: July 18, 2081
- T. Midpoint: April 23, 2084
- Easter: March 26, 2084
- Yom Kippur: October 5, 2087
- Removal of AofD: November 4, 2087
- Hanukkah: December 19, 2087
- Yom Kippur to Hanukkah: 75 Days

2081-2088 Timeline: No

- T. Start: October 31, 2081
- D. Sacrifice Start: July 8, 2082
- T. Midpoint: April 13, 2085
- Easter: April 15, 2085
- Yom Kippur: September 24, 2088
- Removal of AofD: October 24, 2088
- Hanukkah: December 7, 2088
- Yom Kippur to Hanukkah: 74 Days

2082-2089 Timeline: No

- T. Start: October 20, 2082
- D. Sacrifice Start: June 27, 2083
- T. Midpoint: April 2, 2086
- Easter: March 31, 2086
- Yom Kippur: September 13, 2089
- Removal of AofD: October 13, 2089
- Hanukkah: November 27, 2089
- Yom Kippur to Hanukkah: 75 Days

2083-2090 Timeline: No

- T. Start: November 9, 2083
- D. Sacrifice Start: July 16, 2084
- T. Midpoint: April 22, 2087
- Easter: April 20, 2087
- Yom Kippur: October 3, 2090
- Removal of AofD: November 2, 2090
- Hanukkah: December 16, 2090
- Yom Kippur to Hanukkah: 74 Days

2084-2091 Timeline: No

- T. Start: October 27, 2084
- D. Sacrifice Start: July 4, 2085
- T. Midpoint: April 9, 2088
- Easter: April 11, 2088
- Yom Kippur: September 21, 2091
- Removal of AofD: October 21, 2091
- Hanukkah: December 5, 2091
- Yom Kippur to Hanukkah: 75 Days

2085-2092 Timeline: No

- T. Start: November 16, 2085
- D. Sacrifice Start: July 24, 2086
- T. Midpoint: April 29, 2089
- Easter: April 3, 2089
- Yom Kippur: October 10, 2092
- Removal of AofD: November 9, 2092
- Hanukkah: December 23, 2092
- Yom Kippur to Hanukkah: 74 Days

2086-2093 Timeline: No

- T. Start: November 5, 2086
- D. Sacrifice Start: July 13, 2087
- T. Midpoint: April 18, 2090
- Easter: April 16, 2090
- Yom Kippur: September 29, 2093
- Removal of AofD: October 29, 2093
- Hanukkah: December 13, 2093
- Yom Kippur to Hanukkah: 75 Days

2087-2094 Timeline: No

- T. Start: October 26, 2087
- D. Sacrifice Start: July 2, 2088
- T. Midpoint: April 8, 2091
- Easter: April 8, 2091
- Yom Kippur: September 19, 2094
- Removal of AofD: October 19, 2094
- Hanukkah: December 2, 2094
- Yom Kippur to Hanukkah: 74 Days

2088-2095 Timeline: No

- T. Start: November 12, 2088
- D. Sacrifice Start: July 20, 2089
- T. Midpoint: April 25, 2092
- Easter: March 30, 2092
- Yom Kippur: October 7, 2095
- Removal of AofD: November 6, 2095
- Hanukkah: December 20, 2095
- Yom Kippur to Hanukkah: 74 Days

2089-2096 Timeline: No

- T. Start: November 1, 2089
- D. Sacrifice Start: July 9, 2090
- T. Midpoint: April 14, 2093
- Easter: April 12, 2093
- Yom Kippur: September 25, 2096
- Removal of AofD: October 25, 2096
- Hanukkah: December 9, 2096
- Yom Kippur to Hanukkah: 75 Days

2090-2097 Timeline: Yes

- T. Start: October 22, 2090
- D. Sacrifice Start: June 29, 2091
- T. Midpoint: April 4, 2094
- Easter: April 4, 2094
- Yom Kippur: September 15, 2097
- Removal of AofD: October 15, 2097
- Hanukkah: November 29, 2097
- Yom Kippur to Hanukkah: 75 Days

2091-2098 Timeline: No

- T. Start: November 11, 2091
- D. Sacrifice Start: July 18, 2092
- T. Midpoint: April 24, 2095
- Easter: April 24, 2095
- Yom Kippur: October 5, 2098
- Removal of AofD: November 4, 2098
- Hanukkah: December 18, 2098
- Yom Kippur to Hanukkah: 74 Days

2092-2099 Timeline: No

- T. Start: October 29, 2092
- D. Sacrifice Start: July 6, 2093
- T. Midpoint: April 11, 2096
- Easter: April 15, 2096
- Yom Kippur: September 23, 2099
- Removal of AofD: October 23, 2099
- Hanukkah: December 6, 2099
- Yom Kippur to Hanukkah: 74 Days

Notes

1. As I stated in the End Time Reckoning chapter, I got dates of holidays at timeanddate.com.

    I account for the fact that Jewish dates begin at sundown. As a result, the dates for Yom Kippur and Hanukkah shown in this book are one day earlier than on timeanddate.com. For instance, the website lists Yom Kippur on October 3, 2033. However, Yom Kippur will start on October 2 at sundown and continue until sundown on October 3.

About the Author

Wayne Croley is a Bible prophecy researcher and commentator from Sacramento, California.

He has studied and written extensively about Bible prophecy since he was a teenager with the goal of helping people understand current events and the truth about the end times.

Wayne is the founder of *Prophecy Proof Insights*, a Bible prophecy website attracting readers from across the globe.

He is also the author of *Prophecy Proof Insights on the End Times*, a comprehensive book about the end times.

Wayne holds an MBA from the California State University, Sacramento. He also holds a degree in Managerial Economics (graduating with highest honors) and a degree in Political Science (graduating with high honors) from the University of California, Davis.

Wayne is also a winner of the prestigious Clyde Jacobs and Larry Peterman Distinguished Scholar Award.

Made in the USA
Middletown, DE
18 December 2022